THE ESSENTIAL

BACKPACKER

THE ESSENTIAL
BACK

PACKER

A Complete Guide for the Foot Traveler

ADRIENNE HALL

RAGGED MOUNTAIN PRESS / McGRAW-HILL

CAMDEN, MAINE • NEW YORK • SAN FRANCISCO • WASHINGTON, D.C. • AUCKLAND
BOGOTÁ • CARACAS • LISBON • LONDON • MADRID • MEXICO CITY • MILAN
MONTREAL • NEW DELHI • SAN JUAN • SINGAPORE • SYDNEY • TOKYO • TORONTO

Ragged Mountain Press
A Division of The McGraw-Hill Companies

10 9 8 7 6 5 4 3 2 1

Copyright © 2001 Ragged Mountain Press

All rights reserved. The publisher takes no responsibility for the use of any of the materials or methods described in this book, nor for the products thereof. The name "Ragged Mountain Press" and the Ragged Mountain Press logo are trademarks of The McGraw-Hill Companies. Printed in the United States of America.

Library of Congress Cataloging-in-Publication Data
Hall, Adrienne.
    The essential backpacker : a complete guide for the foot traveler / Adrienne Hall.
        p.   cm.
    Includes index.
    ISBN 0-07-135437-9 (alk. paper)
    1. Backpacking. 2. Hiking. I. Title: Complete guide for the foot traveler. II. Title.
    GV199.6.H36 2001
    796.51—dc21   00-045891

Questions regarding the content of this book should be addressed to
Ragged Mountain Press
P.O. Box 220
Camden, ME 04843
www.raggedmountainpress.com

Questions regarding the ordering of this book should be addressed to
The McGraw-Hill Companies
Customer Service Department
P.O. Box 547
Blacklick, OH 43004
Retail customers: 1-800-262-4729
Bookstores: 1-800-722-4726

This book is printed on 70# Citation by R. R. Donnelley, Crawfordsville, IN

Design by Dede Cummings
Production management by Janet Robbins
Page layout by Deborah Evans
Edited by Tom McCarthy and Allen Gooch
Photographs by the author unless otherwise noted.
Illustrations on pages 83-85 by William Hamilton, all other illustrations by Elayne Sears. Photos by the author except for the following: pages 96 and 98 Cheyenne Rouse; pages 12, 92 and 94 Stephanie Hager. Map page 89 courtesy of Natural Resources Conservation Service/United States Department of Agriculture.

Band-Aid, Caladryl, Coleman, Counter Assault, Gore-Tex, Lexan, Mace, Neosporin, Sawyer Venom Extractor, and Sno-Seal are registered trademarks.

THE ESSENTIAL

BACKPACKER

CONTENTS

BACKPACKING 301: EXPANDING YOUR HORIZONS — **87**

INTRODUCTION

You wake from a deep, comfortable sleep, and for a moment you can't remember where you are. You reach up and unzip the door of the tent. You squint into the sun and recall yesterday's climb that brought you to this emerald lake. Except for a chirping bird and the occasional splash of a fish, it is silent. You are at home. You make a cup of coffee and pack your gear. Everything you need fits comfortably on your back. There are no rules today: no clocks, no phones, no deadlines, no commitments. The only responsibility you have is to yourself—that is, to go wherever your feet take you and do whatever your heart desires. Such are the joys of backpacking.

WHAT IS BACKPACKING?

The two components of backpacking are hiking and spending the night in the woods. Backpacking involves hiking with enough food and equipment to live in the backcountry for whatever amount of time you desire. Backpackers are self-supporting, carrying their house, kitchen, bed, and bathroom wherever they travel. They are free, limited only by their sense of adventure and bound only by their goals and ambitions.

Backpacking allows you to travel to destinations that many other recreationists cannot get to. Many of the most magnificent places on the planet are inaccessible by car, truck, motorcycle, or bicycle. As a backpacker, you *experience* the landscape; you don't see it as a blur through a windshield. It makes no difference if your final destination is an alpine lake, a grassy bluff, a sandy spit beside a river, or a stand of old-growth redwoods. As a self-sufficient backpacker, you can travel to whatever destination you have in mind.

ABOUT THE AUTHOR

I was lucky. My parents took me hiking and camping regularly throughout grade school. When I embarked on my own adventures and set out on longer trips in unfamiliar places, I made a lot of mistakes. Actually, I prefer to say that I created a lot of challenges for myself. I learned largely by trial and error. As with any outdoor adventure, the trips that didn't turn out as expected became some of the most memorable experiences of my life.

When I hiked the 2,159-mile Appalachian National Scenic Trail from Georgia to Maine, I spent six months creating challenges for myself and making many mistakes. Those misadventures, as well as some of the most incredible experiences of my life, are documented in a book called *A Journey North: One Woman's Story of Hiking the Appalachian Trail*. A few years later, I refined my skills even further during a continuous hike of the 500-mile Colorado Trail from Denver to Durango. I tried different techniques for reducing my pack weight, and I experimented with more creative backcountry cuisine.

I certainly don't have it all figured out, but I do have a number of miles behind me and the experiences, good and bad, that come with those miles. Just as there are many ways to get from Point A to Point B, there are innumerable ways to make the experience more enjoyable. There is no one right way to backpack. Everyone has a different style, and I continue to learn from everyone I meet.

Over the years, I've shared with friends my successes and failures and have introduced a number of people to the sport. *The Essential Backpacker* offers you the same tutorial, taking you through the ins and outs of hiking and backpacking until you feel confident setting off on your own.

IS IT FOR YOU?

I have always felt more comfortable in wild places than in urban areas. Watching a sliver of moon rise above a jagged ridge, listening to a whisper of wind slip across a lake, or wading through wildflowers up to my waist provides the thrill, the sense of self-awareness, and the peace that enhances the rest of my life. Backpacking has made me feel confident in other aspects of my life, it has helped me become physically stronger, and it has allowed me to relax and be in the presence of beautiful things. You may want to backpack to get in shape, to test your limits, to explore a new area, or to share a bonding experience with family and friends. You may want to backpack to access fishing or hunting opportunities, to photograph wildlife or paint natural landscapes, or to sharpen your birding or tracking skills.

I've met backpackers who started when they were infants and others who started in their sixties, once they retired and had more free time. I've met parents who backpack with small children, college students who crave the feeling of standing on top of a mountain, pregnant women who enjoy the exercise, couples who seek solace in nature from a stressful week at work, and men and women well into their eighties who are not content with sitting and rocking away the rest of their lives. If you can walk, and if you have an adventurous spirit, you can backpack. It's that simple.

Of course, you are bound to face some challenges—a steep climb, a rainy night, or a river crossing—and you need to develop the skills to address those challenges. This book will teach you the skills you need to ensure that your backpacking experiences are safe, comfortable, and fun.

HOW TO USE THIS BOOK

When I started backpacking, I didn't have a book or an instructor to make the path more navigable. But you do. By sharing with you the tricks of the trail, and by outlining skills and techniques in a clear, concise style, I hope to make your trips, as well as your learning experience, enjoyable.

This book is designed as a course. It begins with day trips and familiarizes you with the basics of hiking: where to go, how to get started, what you need to bring. The second part introduces you to backpacking—that is, hiking and spending at least one night in the woods. It includes sections on gear selection and preparations for backpacking, strategies for setting up camp, cooking tips, route-finding skills, and ways to minimize your impact on the environment, and it introduces you to skills and techniques to enhance your safety and comfort in the backcountry. The third part of the course is designed to set the stage for more advanced experiences like hiking with children, taking your dog, backpacking long distances, and backpacking in different seasons and in more severe conditions.

This guide is helpful for those who are just beginning and for the advanced backpacker who wants to refine his or her skills. There is always room to improve. Reading this book is one way. The most important way, however, is to get out there and practice. Embrace the challenge. You can do it! Right here, right now is a good place to start.

A WALK IN THE WOODS

The first part of this course will prepare you for day hiking. If you already hike, consider yourself ahead of the game, but read this part closely, for it is critical to have the right gear and have your day-hiking skills honed to perfection before you embark on an overnighter.

Become comfortable with hiking. Experiment with different kinds of boots and packs. Try hiking in the rain, in the height of summer, by yourself, or in an unfamiliar place. Practice the techniques as you learn them. With every hike, you will feel more comfortable and confident in wild places. Soon you will be ready to spend a night in the woods.

WHAT YOU WILL NEED

Before you set out on a day hike, you will need to acquire some hiking gear. You'll need a backpack, hiking boots, and proper clothing, and you'll need to bring adequate food and water. These items are essential because they help keep you warm, dry, healthy, and comfortable. Keep in mind, however, that equipping yourself for a day hike does not require a major investment. Lightweight hiking boots range from $30 to $90, a daypack can be purchased for as little as $20, and an inexpensive rainjacket costs between $30 and $60. Although high-end equipment will cost a bit more, don't feel obligated to buy anything fancy for a day hike. In fact, a pair of sneakers, a borrowed backpack, and a plastic poncho will suffice for your first outing.

With a good attitude, there's no such thing as a bad hiking trip!

ATTITUDE: THE MOST IMPORTANT THING YOU CARRY

The most important thing you will take on any hike is neither the backpack nor the boots, but a positive attitude. You must be flexible and willing to change your plans. If you get a blister, hike a shorter distance. If you discover a new trail and wonder where it goes, follow it. Venture into the woods with the understanding that nature is unpredictable. So are trail conditions. Be prepared to change your plans if a thunderstorm comes out of nowhere or if you discover a campsite too beautiful to pass up. Also be prepared to modify your trip to accommodate the goals and abilities of the people you are hiking with. Understand that you can prepare for many conditions and situations, but you can't fully control your outdoor experience. Take it as it comes, and make the most of whatever comes your way.

After all, overcoming obstacles, embracing the challenge, and responding to ever-changing conditions are what make hiking rewarding. If the trails I've hiked were always flat and smooth, the sky always sunny, the gear always working perfectly, I wouldn't have felt half as accomplished at the end of the day. Remember, you are outside, doing what you want to do, living fully and completely. For those reasons, it is worth it.

No matter what circumstances present themselves, you can always have a good time if you set your mind to it. There are no bad conditions, just bad attitudes. So relinquish your control, put away your pride, bury your competitive edge, and remember this important advice: if you can laugh at yourself, you will always have successful hiking trips. A sense of humor should be your most treasured possession.

DAYPACKS

No matter how far you plan to hike, you will need something in which to carry the rest of your gear. Small backpacks, called *daypacks*, are found in most outfitters and department stores. I like to carry the backpack I used in school. It is big enough for warm clothes, snacks, and 2 quarts of water. It has two external pouches and a top pouch for storing items that I want at my fingertips, like a camera, sunglasses, and lip balm.

Daypacks come in a variety of models. Choose one that's simple and comfortable.

I highly recommend carrying a daypack that has a built-in foam pad so that sharp or uneven objects won't jab you in the back as you walk. A daypack with a small hipbelt will be more comfortable to carry. Padded shoulder straps are a must. Be wary of packs that have a lot of loops and straps and pockets; these add-ons are helpful only if you need them. If not, they will get in the way and increase the price of the pack.

BOOTS

If your feet hurt, you won't be going far, which is why comfortable footwear is imperative. When you're searching for the right shoe or boot, keep in mind that your feet are unique and that what fits your best friend may not necessarily work best

Lightweight hiking boots are ideal for day hikes and backpacking trips on gentle terrain.

Footwear: Find the Right Fit

In fall 1995, I began planning for a continuous hike of the 2,159-mile Appalachian Trail, which traverses the spine of the Appalachian range from Georgia to Maine. Guidebooks recommended preparing for the trek at least three months in advance. That winter I began assembling food, getting in shape, and selecting gear. Convinced that I needed a bombproof boot for such a long trip, I marched down to the outdoor outfitter and came back with a pair of leather boots that had a full metal shank and a high cut. Each boot weighed 3 pounds. The boots were so solid

they didn't bend when I walked; I felt as though I had wooden planks strapped to my feet.

On the trail, the boots kept my feet dry and provided considerable ankle support, but the leather was not getting softer. After a week of hiking, I acquired severe blisters and had to wrap my feet in moleskin and foam pads. The blisters lingered for over a month. It took almost five months of hiking for my boots to feel comfortable. If I had to do it over again, I would select a lightweight, less rigid boot, or I would spend more than three months breaking in a sturdy pair.

A few years later, when I set off to hike the 500-mile Colorado Trail, which traverses a high-elevation region from Denver to Durango, I chose a lightweight pair of boots and was considerably more comfortable. The terrain of the Colorado Trail is not as steep and rocky as is the terrain along the Appalachian Trail, and I encountered much drier weather, which meant that it wasn't critical to have waterproof footwear. I think it's important to consider the type of terrain and the weather conditions when selecting a boot, but comfort ought to be the number one consideration.

for you. I recommend choosing the lightest shoe in which you can comfortably hike. For people with strong ankles, or for people who will hike primarily on smooth terrain, a trail-running shoe or a sneaker might be appropriate. But if you want a bit more support and a bit more padding between your soles and the rocks, opt for a lightweight hiking boot. Depending on your budget, you may choose a less expensive fabric boot ($30–$90) or a higher priced leather or waterproof boot ($100–$180). These particulars are a matter of personal preference. Every boot can be treated with a conditioner to enhance its water-resistant character.

Your boot ought to rise above your ankle, and it ought to fit. This sounds silly, but proper fit is often difficult to come by. You should have enough room in the front of the boot to wriggle your toes, the tongue should lie comfortably across the top of your foot, and the heel should feel snug. When you're trying on boots, wear the thick wool or synthetic socks you plan on wearing during your hike. If you think you've found a good fit, see how it feels after you've worn the boot around the store for a half hour. A properly fitted boot should still feel comfortable after hours of use.

After you've made a purchase, you'll need to break in your boots. Nothing is worse than getting blisters on the trail after the first mile. Increase the time you spend in your new boots until you can comfortably walk all day in them.

CLOTHING

As you think about clothing for a day hike, let me recommend that you start with what you have in your closet. You may find that you have everything you need: it's just a matter of choosing the right items. Think loose and comfortable.

Although your choice of clothing depends largely on where you're going, there are a few fundamental principles for clothing selection. First, leave the cotton T-shirts and jeans at home. Even if it doesn't rain, your clothes will get wet from perspiration, and wet shirts and jeans will quickly become heavy and uncomfortable. You don't want to be caught in the woods in wet cotton when the temperature drops. Cotton takes forever to dry, and even on a warm day you can easily catch a chill in a wet cotton shirt.

Synthetic materials, on the other hand, wick moisture away from your skin, allow your skin to breathe, and provide warmth even when wet. Silk, wool, and synthetic materials such as poly propylene and polyester microfleece are all good choices.

When you dress for a hike, think about wrapping your body in different layers. Starting with the layer closest to their skin, many hikers wear synthetic underwear and a sports bra made of anything but cotton. In warmer climes, I wear a tank top and quick-drying shorts, and I bring a fleece jacket just in case it cools off. On cooler days, I wear a polypropylene long-sleeve shirt underneath a lightweight fleece top. Synthetic long-underwear pants or baggy climbing slacks are good choices for your bottom half.

Rain is an unavoidable fact of life for every hiker. Keep in mind one rule of thumb no matter what the sky looks like when you leave your house: never leave home without a rainjacket. I live in the mountains where the weather changes quickly, so even on the sunniest days I carry a waterproof rainjacket in my daypack.

On all my backwoods jaunts, I add a hat and gloves to my hiking gear. These items take up almost no room in my pack, and they are much appreciated when the wind picks up or the skies look threatening. A bandanna is another good addition to any hiker's daypack. Use it as a headband or to towel off in a stream.

A final note on clothing: don't neglect your feet. If you cover them with care, they will treat you well. Most important, never wear cotton socks on a hike. Cotton is a good prescription for blisters because it traps moisture and sticks to your skin. A silk or synthetic liner sock worn under a heavier wool or synthetic sock is your best bet. A liner sock will wick moisture away from your foot and allow the heavier sock, as well as the boot, to slide across the liner sock as you walk. This prevents friction against your skin, so your feet will stay blister-free!

GEAR FOR A DAY HIKE

Before you set off on a hike, consider tossing a few other items into your pack. First of all, get used to carrying a map and compass. "But I'm only going on the trail by my house," you say. "I've been there a hundred times." Then that is the perfect area to learn how to use the map and compass. That way, if you get confused when you're reading the compass, you won't panic. Learn how to stay found before you get lost (more information on map and compass skills is on pages 56 to 59).

In sunny or snowy areas, never leave home without sunscreen, sunglasses, and lip balm. Spending all day in the sun with no protection is un-healthy and can be painful.

Take a scaled-down version of a first-aid kit on all day hikes. You can never predict when you or someone around you is going to scrape a knee or twist an ankle, so it's always better to be pre-pared. Ninety-nine percent of the time, I use my first-aid kit to treat and prevent blisters. For blisters I carry precut moleskin (that sticky, fuzzy stuff that you can get at any drugstore or pharmaceutical section of the grocery store) or molefoam and adhesive tape; for scrapes I carry antibiotic ointment and Band-Aids. I carry an elastic bandage for wrapping a knee, ankle, or elbow, and I take a small pocketknife or scissors to cut tape or bandages.

Depending on where you are hiking and what your interests are, you may want to include many of the following items in your daypack: insect repellent, field guide and binoculars, hand lens for identifying wildflowers, camera, notebook, and pen. What you decide to bring is up to you. Consider your goals. What will make you happy? Some people don't want to be bothered with anything except a jacket and wa-ter; others fill their packs with field guides and camera lenses.

The next two items are again a matter of personal preference. Many hikers like to wear an-kle gaiters, which are a shorter,

lighter, cooler version of full-length gaiters. Gaiters consist of a piece of material that wraps around your calf to keep dirt, debris, or snow from getting into the top of your boot. Gaiters also protect your legs from scrapes or deep snow. They are very handy, weigh almost nothing, and prevent you

In addition to food, water, and a rainjacket, you may want to bring a camera, guidebooks, and a first-aid kit on a day hike.

from having to stop every few minutes to shake a pebble out of your boot. When hiking off-trail, I consider gaiters an essential piece of clothing, but on easy to moderate hikes I rarely wear them.

I urge you not to laugh at my final recommendation: an umbrella. It seems like a silly thing to bring along, but I can tell you firsthand that, as long as you're not on a windy, exposed ridge or in very dense vegetation, an umbrella will keep you far drier than a rainjacket will. If you don't mind people staring at you (after all, it is quite a sight to see someone hiking with an umbrella!), and if you don't mind holding on to something when you walk, consider bringing one along. I know, I too was a disbeliever, but now I'm a full-fledged, umbrella-carrying hiker. (See appendix 1 for an equipment checklist for a day hike.)

SNACKS FOR THE TRAIL

Items that will keep you warm and dry are essential for a day hike, but you'll also need energy to sustain yourself for an afternoon of trekking through the woods. To fuel your body for a hike, you may want to pack a picnic lunch. After all, lunch is a good excuse to stop, rest, and enjoy the scenery. If an all-out lunch is not your style, pack snacks for the trail. Always have some food at your fingertips to replenish the reserves.

On a backpacking trip, you will want to bring food that is lightweight, compact, and nonperishable. You can bring the same types of food items on a day hike; it is good practice for your longer trips. I like to take fruit, nuts, an energy bar, and jerky. You may like cheese and crackers, a peanut butter sandwich, or corn chips. Repackage whatever food you decide to take—there's no need to take the entire box of crackers and an enormous hunk of cheese. And what if it rains or your pack gets stepped on? You end up with soggy cracker crumbs in your pack.

Put the amount of food you will eat in a resealable plastic bag. That way you can reseal the bag and keep the food clean and dry and free from bugs.

Enjoy your snacks, but be sure to pack out whatever you pack in. That means the apple core, peanut shells, and, of course, candy wrappers. I carry an extra resealable bag for trash.

WATER

Staying hydrated is extremely important. On a hike, you have two options: bring water with you or treat it as you go. You can treat water by boiling it, by using iodine, or by filtering it (water-treatment methods are discussed on pages 43 to 45). These methods can be time-consuming and require that you carry more gear, so on a day hike it is usually easier to bring all the water you need and leave the stove and water filter at home.

A widemouthed Lexan water bottle.

I prefer to carry two 1-quart, widemouthed water jugs on day hikes. Sure, you can reuse a plastic soda bottle, but know that they are not meant to last forever. Some hikers prefer cyclists' water bottles. They are easy to drink from but are far from indestructible. Be wary of the pull-up spouts; they almost always leak. The last thing you want is a wet daypack filled with wet gear.

A water bottle with a screw-on top is your best bet. A reliable choice is a bottle made of Lexan, a material that won't break and won't retain odors of the things you put into it. That means that on a warm day, water from your Lexan bottle won't taste like plastic—a major bonus! Widemouthed water bottles can be found at any outfitter or sporting goods store.

What happens if you accidentally spill the water? Instead of going thirsty for the rest of the day, or taking your chances by drinking water directly from the river, you can refill your jug in the nearest creek if you have iodine tablets. A tiny bottle of iodine tablets is inexpensive ($7) and can be found at any outfitting or sporting goods store. Toss a tablet in your jug, let it dissolve for about twenty minutes, and your water will be safe to drink. Keep a tiny bottle of iodine tablets in your first-aid kit. You may never need it, but it's good peace of mind to know that you don't have to go thirsty.

PLANNING

Deciding where to go is often the most difficult part of the hiking experience, not because finding a place is difficult (quite the contrary), but because there are so many places to choose from. On my refrigerator, I keep a list of places and trails that I hope to visit. My list never gets shorter, because I keep adding trails. On every new hike I seem to find three or four other trails I'd like to venture down. You may want to start a similar list.

WHERE TO GO

Not sure where to begin? No problem. The first thing you ought to do is go to your local outdoor outfitter and consult the people who sell hiking and camping gear. Look in the yellow pages of your phone book under sporting goods, mountain climbing equipment, or camping equipment. The people who work in these stores should know the area, the trails, and the best times to go. They can offer numerous suggestions, sell you maps, and help you plan your trip. Your list will grow in no time.

The search for a hiking area doesn't have to begin and end at the outfitting store. There are many other ways to find the ideal hiking spot in your neck of the woods. Begin your search by contacting agencies like the local chamber of commerce or bureau of tourism. Consult the four federal agencies that manage public land: U.S. Forest Service, National Park Service, Bureau of Land Management (BLM), and Fish and Wildlife Service.

The bureau of tourism or chamber of commerce nearest you can tell you which national park is closest to your home. If a national park is too far away for a day hike, try a state park. In the western United States, BLM land is abundant and often overlooked when planning trips; solitude is easy to come by and you typically won't need to fuss with permits. National wildlife refuges are excellent places to recreate, and you'll often have a good chance of encountering wildlife.

Consider joining a local hiking club or outing club, where you'll meet people with similar interests and be able to share ideas for upcoming adventures. Conservation organizations like the Sierra Club, the Nature Conservancy, and the Audubon Society offer guided hikes and provide an opportunity to learn a little natural history of your area. Joining a trail maintenance club (usually associated with a hiking club) is another terrific way to get involved because you'll work with people who know a lot about trails. If you're lucky, they'll share some of their favorite places with you. (See appendix 5 for contact information for clubs and organizations.)

Still searching? Get ideas for trips from magazines, the Internet, and mapping companies. Magazines such as *Backpacker*, *Outside*, or *National Geographic Traveler* have a destination section that highlights trails in various geographic regions. Many World Wide Web sites such as those listed in appendix 5 offer ideas for hiking destinations and even provide maps and trail descriptions. Obtain a map from one of the many mapping companies (see appendix 5) and come up with a plan of your own. For example, the Earth Science Information Center (ESIC) collects and assembles information from local, state, and federal government agencies and is an excellent source of topographic maps.

ENVIRONMENT

What type of scenery are you looking for? Do you want to walk along a river? To the top of a mountain or a scenic overlook? To a meadow? To a cave? To a historic cabin? Around a lake? Along a beach? When you think about hiking, where do you picture yourself? In a dense forest? In an alpine meadow? Surrounded by rocky peaks? Strolling across a mesa? Picking your way along a desert trail?

For a day hike, you probably want to choose someplace close to home, but even within your local environment there is probably some variation. Think about where you want to spend your day. Also consider your ability. If you are beginning, avoid long, steep hikes in unfamiliar places. Choose well-marked trails and avoid areas that are not clearly marked, appear to be unused, or seem very rugged. A hike along a river or on a popular 4-mile loop in a state park may be a good choice.

Time and Terrain

Consider how much time you can devote to the hike because the amount of time you have will determine how far you can go. Obviously, people walk at different speeds; only you know how quickly you can travel. As a general guideline, people tend to hike at a pace of about 2 miles per hour. If you take a lot of rest breaks or stop often to look at flowers or rocks, you'll need to factor in a little more time to get to your destination.

One important factor in hiking is the terrain; covering 3 miles on a flat trail will be drastically different from traveling 3 miles up the side of a rocky mountain!

There are three main types of terrain: gentle, moderate, and rugged. Gentle terrain refers to a trail or a landscape that is relatively free of obstacles like rocks and unforgiving vegetation. Gentle terrain is flat, or nearly so. Moderate terrain is a bit more challenging, involving some ups and downs and possibly some roots and rocks that you'll have to negotiate. Rugged terrain can be quite steep, exposed to the elements, or unclearly marked or can involve rocky scrambles. You can have excellent experiences in all three types of terrain. Don't think you have to strive for the most technical ascent and the most grueling trail. Select terrain that best suits your personality, your abilities, and your goals for the day.

Once you've considered the terrain and the time you have, gauge the distance accordingly. If the terrain is relatively flat and smooth, you can cover longer distances. If a number of climbs are involved in your day, plan on hiking at a slower pace. For example, if you want to walk for three hours, choose a gentle 5-mile walk around a lake (remember, you probably won't be walking for all three hours, so factor in time for breaks), or choose a 3-mile jaunt up and down steep hills. As always, consider your physical ability. What takes one person an hour may take the next person two hours.

Goals

The length of your hike, the terrain you select, and the location of your hike ought to match your goals. Choose a season and a time of day that are

The Day I Tortured My Mother

After spending one summer in Colorado, I had fallen in love with the Rockies. My parents, who lived in Pennsylvania, would receive weekly updates of my adventures: glissading down snowy chutes on the slopes of 13,000-foot mountains, walking through meadows of wildflowers up to my waist, and waking in the morning to the sound of bugling elk. When my mother said she wanted to visit me and see where I lived, I was thrilled at the prospect of sharing a slice of the Rockies with her. I wanted her to understand how exhilarating it was to climb above the tree line and feel the sun burning through the thin air on the Rocky Mountain ridges. I thought that if I took her on a hike, she would understand why this place was so important to me and why I wanted to live like that for the rest of my life.

At the end of the summer, my mother came to visit. I had heard about a hike to natural hot springs below a snow-lined rocky cirque. Perfect. The scenery up there would certainly astound her. I couldn't wait. On my map, the trail looked like a moderate 10-mile walk, but a couple miles into the trip, it became apparent that I hadn't carefully studied the route or considered my mother's ability level. The trail was steep and rocky and climbed over a 13,000-foot pass. My mother, who had come from sea level, huffed and puffed her way to the pass. The level dirt path quickly dissolved into a rocky scramble that traversed precipitous ledges. Mom almost gave up when we had to cross a snowfield, but as dark thunderheads gathered overhead, I pleaded with her to continue. A hike to the hot springs, which I thought would take about five hours, took ten. The trail was really about 15 miles long, and the elevation and rugged terrain slowed our pace. Exhausted and out of food and water, we returned to the car in total darkness.

Fortunately, my mother is a hardy soul and a good sport; now she just laughs when she recalls the time I took her on a "death march." Realizing what a dangerous situation I had put us in, I now spend more time before hikes studying topo maps and talking with people who know the area to verify mileage, elevation changes, and the type of terrain.

Gentle terrain provides excellent backpacking opportunities, especially for beginners.

appropriate for the area and consistent with your objectives. If you hope to observe wildlife, hike closer to dusk or dawn. If you want to climb an exposed ridge but don't want to make it too hard on yourself, do it before the first snow. If you are trekking through the desert and want to be comfortable, avoid midsummer and the heat of the day. Common sense will go a long way when deciding when and where to hike.

The best thing you can do once you've narrowed things down is to speak with someone who has been there. Now is the time to go to outfitters, rangers, or naturalists and find out what they have to say about the area. In addition to helping you match an area to your goals, they can inform you about current trail conditions and things to pay particular attention to, like a pair of nesting eagles, or a missing trail marker, or a shortcut to the trailhead.

You are ready. You have boots that fit, a comfortable pack in which to carry your gear, and adequate food and water. You've selected a trail that is appropriate for the amount of time you have, your abilities, and your goals. You've obtained a map and consulted someone about your choice. It's time to get out there and have a great time. Grab a friend and go for it!

Rugged terrain is often steep and rocky. Allow extra time when traversing challenging sections of trail.

A NIGHT IN THE WOODS

Congratulations. You've done it. You've embarked on a day hike or two, you've become comfortable with the process of selecting a route and choosing gear, and you understand what it takes to achieve your goals. You also probably have begun to realize both the physical and the mental benefits of hiking. Now you're ready to challenge yourself and take it to the next level: you're ready to make the transition from day hiking to backpacking. The following information will help you plan and prepare for a backpacking trip. I've included information on gear selection, safety precautions, personal hygiene, food preparation, and backcountry skills and techniques to ensure that your travels are safe and rewarding. As you invest more time and energy in backpacking trips, the rewards you reap will be greater, too.

THE BASICS

Eighty years ago, backpackers didn't have the luxuries we have today. They carried packs with little support, slept under wool blankets, and hiked in flimsy shoes. Fortunately, the surge in popularity of outdoor recreation has driven the outdoor industry to create backpacking gear that maximizes comfort and efficiency. We have waterproof tents, luxuriously padded backpacks, stoves that are a cinch to light, and sleeping bags that weigh only a couple of pounds and that keep you toasty on even the most frigid nights. Because there is so much equipment to choose from, deciding what you need for a backpacking trip can be a bit overwhelming. This section will help you decide exactly what you need to bring to make the most of your trip.

FOOTWEAR

Anyone who has ever hiked with wet, cold, or blistered feet can attest to the importance of quality footwear. Your feet will take a lot of abuse on a backpacking trip, so do everything you can to keep them warm, dry, and comfortable. Let's consider footwear a package deal, consisting of socks, boots, and gaiters.

Socks

The socks you wear backpacking can be the same socks you wore on your day hike: a silk or synthetic

Synthetic sock liners (left) *and synthetic or wool hiking socks* (right) *are a good defense against blisters.*

liner under a heavy wool or synthetic hiking sock. On a backpacking trip, I bring two sets; I alternate between the two, wearing one while the other dries. I often strap the dirty pair to the outside of my backpack to let the socks air out while I walk. If I'm feeling decadent, I bring a pair of cozy cotton socks to wear around camp and in the tent on cooler nights. On most summer trips, however, it feels good to let my feet air out at night, so I don't worry about bringing extra camp socks.

Boots

If you're happy with the lightweight boots you wore hiking, you can probably wear them backpacking. I wear the lightest, most comfortable boot that will give me enough support when I'm hiking with a loaded backpack. A light- or midweight boot is ideal. Anything heavier may be overkill. Trust me, after backpacking all day, a 3-pound hiking boot will feel like a 20-pound chunk of lead. Best reserve the heavy boots for snow and ice and more technical adventures.

Fit is the number one priority, so spend some time with the salesperson, and spend some time in the boot. (Boot fit is described on pages 14 to 15.)

To increase the longevity of your boot, invest in a water-repellency treatment. Treatments come in sprays, liquids, or pastes that you massage into the leather or fabric. A few words of caution about treatments. First, the treatment will change the color of the boot—expect the boot to end up a few shades darker. Second, use a treatment designed specifically for the material from which your boot

Midweight or heavyweight hiking boots may be appropriate for backpacking trips, especially if you'll encounter rugged terrain.

was constructed. Treatments vary depending on whether your boot is made from leather, suede, fabric, Gore-Tex, or other materials. For example, you don't want to use a wax-based treatment like Sno-Seal on Gore-Tex. It will clog the pores in the material and render the Gore-Tex useless. Your salesperson can help you find the right treatment. (Techniques for cleaning and storing boots are in appendix 4.)

Gaiters

You've discovered that ankle gaiters can be quite useful on hikes, especially if you have a tendency to kick dirt, sand, or pebbles into your boots. Ankle gaiters can also be invaluable on summer back-packing trips.

For trips through dense brush, or in cold or snowy conditions, try full-length gaiters. They wrap around your leg from your ankle to just below your knee. Not only do they keep debris from getting into your boots, but also they protect your legs from getting scraped by shrubs or snow. If you wrap them tightly enough, you may even be able to ford shallow streams and keep your feet dry as you bound across!

Full-length gaiters.

Increase the life of your boots and enhance their water-resistant capabilities by applying a treatment.

CLOTHING

The outdoor clothing concepts we discussed in Backpacking 101 apply to this section as well. The goal is to create a layering system out of synthetic materials that will keep you warm and dry when it's cold out and that allow you to shed layers and be comfortable when it's hot.

You'll notice that in every subsequent section in this book, the issue of weight enters the picture. Backpackers often become obsessed about the weight of their packs; after a day of shouldering a 40-pound pack, you will quickly understand why. If you can cut a few ounces here, a few ounces there, it will add up. Your pack will weigh less, you will be more comfortable, and you will have a more enjoyable experience. The mission you are charged with is this: bring with you the things that will keep you comfortable for a couple days in the woods without making the pack so heavy that the walking becomes uncomfortable.

Occasionally I've come across backpackers who practice ultralight traveling. To keep their pack weights to a minimum, they'll forgo a tent, sleeping mattress, stove, fuel, and cookware. A lightweight tarp or bivy bag (bivouac bag) replaces a tent, and they sometimes use a small quilt instead of a sleeping bag. All their gear fits into a daypack and can weigh as little as 10 pounds (minus food). While ultralight backpacking may not appeal to everyone, the weight of your gear should always be considered as you select items for a trip.

So, before we talk about how much clothing you should bring on a backpacking trip, let's talk about the things you *don't* need to bring. Most important, you don't need a change of clothes for every day. Yes, you can hike in the same shirt and shorts for three days—it won't kill you, and it doesn't have to be uncomfortable. The trick to staying somewhat clean and fresh is to reserve a change of clothes for the night. Nighttime is the time to break out your favorite cotton T-shirt. Snuggle into your sleeping bag in something that smells clean and your bag will stay cleaner, too.

As mentioned earlier, you should avoid wearing cotton clothing while backpacking. Bulky items such as jeans and sweatshirts occupy a disproportionate amount of space in your pack for the warmth they provide.

The specific items you choose will depend, of course, on your personal preference, where you are backpacking, and the length of the trip. Still, there are a few things to keep in mind. Choose items that allow your legs and arms full range of motion. Wear clothes that have smooth seams; pants with bulky belt loops and shirts that gather beneath pack straps will create bruises or chafing. Your clothes should lie flat and smooth across your body and not cause you any discomfort when you're strapped into a backpack.

The most efficient way to use your clothing is to keep one outfit clean and dry at all times. If you hike all day in an outfit, it will most likely be damp and dirty. On a generally damp or cool evening, I sleep with the damp clothes in my sleeping bag and by morning they are dry. Because it is imperative to have one set of clothes dry at all times, I recommend that you change into your dirty clothes in the morning. If you change into fresh clothes in the morning, they will be fresh and dry for only a few minutes, and then you end up with two sets of dirty, damp clothes. I understand that changing into dirty clothes is not the most pleasant experience, but once you start walking, it won't make a difference.

I strive to be a minimalist. On a four-day trip, here's what I take: one pair of shorts, two shirts to hike in, one shirt to sleep in, two pairs of socks and liners, one fleece jacket, rain pants, a rainjacket, a bandanna, fleece hat, and wool gloves. It is a blessing to lounge around camp at the end of the day and not worry about bugs, especially mosquitoes, so I wear my rain pants and a loose-fitting long-sleeve shirt. You may have a pair of lightweight pants and a favorite shirt that will serve nicely as campwear. Certainly your choice depends on the temperature. On a balmy, 80-degree evening, getting suited up in rain pants and a jacket will not be in your best interest. Bring clothing that seems appropriate for the season and current weather conditions, and always anticipate the nights being a few degrees cooler than you expect.

Where do you put all these clothes? My clothes fit nicely into a stuff sack (a water-resistant bag with a drawstring). I keep differently colored stuff sacks for my clothes, tent, sleeping pad, sleeping bag, and food. That way, when I want my clothes, I know just where to look.

hood with cord
to adjust size
of opening

ventilation
pockets

snug waist

snug cuffs

adjustable
wrist cuffs

storm flap
over front
zipper

room in
knee for
full range
of motion

adjustable
cuffs

*Stay warm and dry by outfitting yourself with a fleece jacket, waterproof jacket,
and synthetic hiking pants.*

BACKPACKS

Backpack design has come a long way from the old canvas rucksacks that didn't have hipbelts to support the load. Fortunately, all modern backpacks have a padded hipbelt that allows you to carry the weight on your hips; padded shoulder straps; and load lifter straps that let you shift the weight between your hips and shoulders. The backpack will be one of your biggest investments, so I recommend borrowing one from a friend or renting one from an outfitter before you buy one.

Packs are divided into two categories: those that have internal frames and those with external frames. Internal-frame packs often have one large main compartment and a top pouch. Proponents of internal-frame packs believe they are very comfortable, provide excellent stability, and are easy to stuff into the trunk of a car or into an overhead bin on an airplane.

External-frame packs went out of vogue for a while but seem to be making a comeback. External-frame packs have many different compartments, and the external frame allows you to strap big items like your tent and sleeping mattress to the outside of the pack. The compartments make it easier to organize gear and more evenly distribute weight. They are designed to facilitate carrying heavy loads, and they are relatively inexpensive ($100 to $200, compared with $150 to $400 for an internal-frame backpack).

Which is better, an internal-frame pack or an external-frame pack? The answer is that it doesn't matter. Choose a pack that fits you. Choose a pack that feels comfortable. Experiment with different brands and spend some time making sure the pack fits. Before you fit the pack, load it with gear from the store. Even the most poorly designed backpack feels comfortable when it's empty! Load the pack with gear from the store that equals about 25 percent of your body weight.

Once the pack is on your back, position the hipbelt so the weight of the pack rests on your skeleton. Don't put the hipbelt too high or too low. If the hipbelt is too high, it will impede your breathing, and if it's too low, it will interfere with your stride. Make sure the pads aren't touching in the front; you want to be able to cinch the hipbelt tightly. Once the hipbelt is secure, tighten the shoulder straps. They should wrap comfortably around your shoulders. Next, tug on the load lifter

Beware the Bothersome Backpack

I'll never forget my first backpack. The salesperson told me that it was designed for women, and when I tried it on in the store and loaded it with 10 pounds, it felt fine. I should have known that even the worst backpack would feel good weighted with only 10 pounds. I was a beginner and didn't know what to look for or how a backpack should feel. I remember being confused by all the straps and figured that I just wouldn't touch them. No one explained the importance of a proper fit or showed me how minor adjustments to the straps could change the way the pack fit on my body.

I bought the backpack and headed into the woods on a number of weekend backpacking trips. After a few miles of walking, the straps would rub uncomfortably on my shoulders and hips. I'd return from every trip with bloody welts on my hipbones and shoulders. I thought this was normal. I figured you had to suffer if you wanted to journey into the wilderness. Like most people, I equated backpacking with aches and pains, sleeping on hard ground, and returning to civilization with a very sore back or, in my case, with chafed hips and shoulders. It wasn't until years later that I experimented

with different backpacks. It soon became clear that my old backpack was not designed for my body. I retired the old pack and purchased a new one that had a beefy hipbelt and shoulder straps that comfortably hugged my shoulders. I learned that by tugging or releasing the load lifter straps near my ears, I could shift the weight of the pack between my hips and shoulders, giving them some relief throughout the day. I learned that backpacking does not mean suffering and that wearing a backpack doesn't have to be agonizing. Needless to say, my trips are far more enjoyable now.

Internal-frame backpack.

straps, which are located next to your ears. Adjusting the load lifter straps will transfer the weight of the pack between your shoulders and your hips, whichever feels more comfortable. Finally, clasp the sternum strap across your chest.

When you walk around the store, the pack should grip your body; it shouldn't be shifting and swinging back and forth. You ought to be able to move your arms and legs freely. You should be able to stand erect without the pack pulling you backward. Make sure the hipbelt and shoulder straps feel snug and comfortable. Notice any spots where the backpack just doesn't feel right. The salesperson can adjust many of the straps to change the way the pack feels. You may want to ask the salesperson to explain exactly what he or she is doing to the pack so you can make adjustments down the

road as you deem necessary. (Techniques for cleaning and storing your backpack are in appendix 4.)

Pack Size

The size of the pack you choose depends on how much space you need to tote your gear. Pack volumes range from 2,000 to 9,000 cubic inches. For most backpacking trips, a 4,000-cubic-inch pack will provide plenty of room for all your equipment. Be wary of superlarge backpacks; all that space seems to encourage you to bring more stuff!

The size of the pack also depends on the length of your torso. Keep in mind that your torso length has nothing to do with your height. With a measuring tape, determine how many inches it is from the bony protrusion at the base of your neck to the

External-frame backpack.

low point between your hipbones. If your torso is fewer than 18 inches, you'll probably take a small suspension system. If your torso is 18 to 20 inches, go with a medium, and a torso longer than 20 usually requires a large suspension system.

Your torso length determines the size of the suspension system, but it doesn't have to affect the volume of the pack. For example, if you have a very small torso but want to carry a huge load, get a backpack with a small suspension system and a large volume, say 6,000 cubic inches.

Pack Fly

Once you've selected the perfect pack, you may want to invest in a pack fly, which is a water-resistant covering for your pack. Most hikers use pack flies, although some prefer to put all their gear in a garbage bag instead. This technique works best with internal-frame packs that have one large compartment. Because garbage bags can be cumbersome and tear easily, I consider a pack fly a good investment.

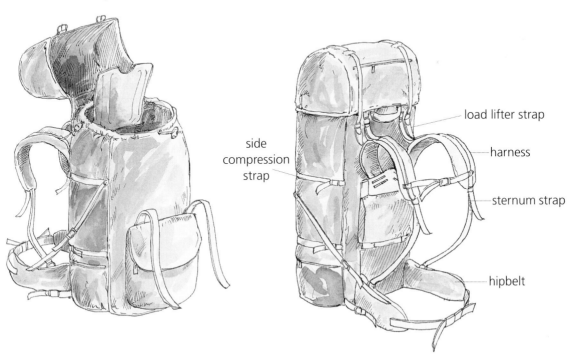

Become familiar with the features of your pack. Adjust the straps to maximize comfort.

SHELTER

Tents

On a clear evening, you may want to kick back in your sleeping bag and sleep under the stars. Some backpackers wouldn't have it any other way. But most backpackers feel more comfortable and secure in some sort of shelter. Although there are alternatives, most backpackers, especially beginners, use a tent. Choosing a tent from the dozens of makes and models can be a nightmare if you don't know what you're looking for. But it doesn't have to be hard. Here are a few suggestions to help you find the tent that's right for you.

First, consider where you will be using the tent. If you'll be camping in hot, dry places and are mainly concerned about sleeping away from the critters, a light summer tent that has a lot of netting will be a good choice. Summer tents are not made to withstand strong rainstorms; they are designed to be well ventilated and let you gaze at the stars.

On the other end of the spectrum are sturdy four-season tents. They are designed to keep you warm and protected from high winds, very low temperatures, and blizzards. They often have an extra pole or two for additional support, which also makes them heavier. For a beginning backpacker, a four-season tent is overkill.

You will probably be most comfortable in a three-season tent. In fact, most tents fall into this category because three-season tents offer the most practical design and function well under most backpacking conditions.

Next, determine how many people will be sleeping in the tent. A two- or three-person tent will suit most people's needs; but if you prefer to be alone or if you have a big family, you may opt for a tent with a smaller or larger capacity. Remember, the larger the tent, the more it will weigh. My two-person, three-season tent weighs about 6 pounds, and that is the most weight I'm willing to allot for a tent.

Price may be your next limiting factor. Tents can range from $100 to $500. Keep in mind that you don't need to buy a tent at the high end of the price range; there are many exceptional $200 tents on the market. If you're trying to keep your costs down, consider buying a used tent.

Once you've narrowed the selection, consider the tent's other features, starting with the vestibule. Most tents have a rainfly—a waterproof covering that shields the tent from the rain—that extends over the doorway to create a covered space outside the tent. This space is called the vestibule. I consider vestibules to be invaluable: they are terrific places to store boots and backpacks, and you don't have to worry about finding a place inside the tent for muddy boots and wet socks. In a downpour, I even cook under the vestibule. Some tents have two doors and two vestibules so you and your partner don't have to crawl over each other to enter and exit the tent. Choose a tent with a vestibule large enough to suit your needs. Do this by erecting the tent in the store and putting two backpacks in the vestibule. You'll soon get an idea of how much space you need.

To ensure that the rainfly remains waterproof, you may have to seal the seams. Many tents come with a tube of seam sealer. If not, pick one up while you're at the store. Seam sealer can be applied to the seams on both the fly and the tent. That way, you'll surely stay dry. (More information on waterproofing your tent can be found on page 52.)

Consider the color. Will the tent blend into the environment? Most hikers prefer a tent that is discreet, while some hikers want a brightly colored tent that will stand out in photographs. Brightly colored tents can be an eyesore, and many rangers consider them a form of visual pollution, so you may be better off in something less flashy.

Many tents have interior pockets and hooks on which you can hang a wet bandanna or a flashlight. Look for a tent that has mesh windows and that is well ventilated. Some tents have a mesh ceiling window that can be covered and zipped shut on cool evenings. Certain features appeal to different people for different reasons. Go with what you like.

Before you buy a tent, learn how to pitch it. That's right, in the store. Don't worry, a salesperson will help you. Pitch the tent and crawl inside. Is the tent what you expected? Is it long enough and

rainfly

tent body

vestibule

A three-season tent with a vestibule is a solid choice for most backpacking trips.

wide enough to accommodate you and your gear? How much does it weigh? Is it easy to set up? This tent will be your home; choose something you'll look forward to climbing into at night.

Ground Cloth

The final component to your shelter is the ground cloth, a piece of waterproof material that lies beneath the tent so the floor of your tent doesn't get wet or get punctured by a stick or stone. Some tents come with a ground cloth that matches the dimensions of the tent floor. Most of the time you'll have to find your own. A piece of 4-millimeter-thick plastic (that you can get at a hardware store) or an old shower curtain will do. Cut the material a few inches smaller than the floor of the tent. If the material extends beyond the tent floor, rain will roll off the rainfly onto the ground cloth and collect under the tent. This is not the way it should

work! A properly cut ground cloth will keep you dry and will extend the life of the tent. (Cleaning and storage techniques for your tent can be found in appendix 4.)

Tarps

I mentioned there are alternatives to using a tent. There are two. The first is a tarp. Some people prefer to get closer to nature than is possible in a tent. For the backpacker who wants a very inexpensive, lightweight shelter, a tarp may be the right choice. A properly strung tarp can shield you from rain and wind, but a tarp comes with drawbacks. It can be difficult to erect because you need properly spaced trees from which to string it. A tarp cannot withstand extreme wind, rain, and snow as a tent can, and a tarp will not protect you from pesky mosquitoes or scurrying mice.

Bivy Bags

Another option is a bivy bag. A bivy bag is a waterproof shell that slips around your sleeping bag. It is easy to transport and certainly doesn't weigh much, but it can cost about as much as a tent. My bivy bag has two small poles that create a little mesh room around my head. This allows me to sit up and read and still be protected from the bugs. Not every bivy bag is equipped with such headroom, however. Because you are confined to a space the size of your sleeping bag, a bivy is not the place to hang out for extended periods. If you like to move around, have your gear with you while you sleep, or play cards with a friend, you'll probably be better off in a tent.

THE BACKPACKER'S BED

Snuggling into a soft, cozy sleeping space at the end of the day ought to be a treat, so make sure your sleeping arrangements provide you with the comfort and warmth you deserve.

Sleeping Bags

Sleeping bags for backpacking are quite different from the rectangular cotton bags you might give your children when you send them to a friend's house for a sleepover. Sleeping bags for backpacking must be lightweight and compact, and they must keep you warm. Old rectangular cotton

Lighten your load with a bivy bag, a good choice for the solo trekker.

bags are none of these things. Modern sleeping bags are often called mummy bags because they are narrow and taper at your feet. This design minimizes the material (and consequently, the weight of the bag) and minimizes the space that your body needs to heat. Thus, you carry a lighter bag and you stay warmer.

A sleeping bag will likely be your bulkiest item, so choose one that compresses into a relatively small stuff sack. My sleeping bag weighs about 3 pounds and fits easily into the bottom of my backpack. The bag you choose will depend on two main factors: the bag's temperature rating and the type of insulation with which the bag is filled.

Sleeping bags are given a temperature rating, the lowest temperature at which the bag will keep you warm. Temperature ratings are approximate because people respond differently to low temperatures. Your response to low temperatures will depend on your body type, your metabolism, what you ate and drank that day, what clothes you're wearing, and how efficient your tent and sleeping mattress are. Still, the temperature rating can provide a rough estimate and give you a place to start when narrowing down the selection.

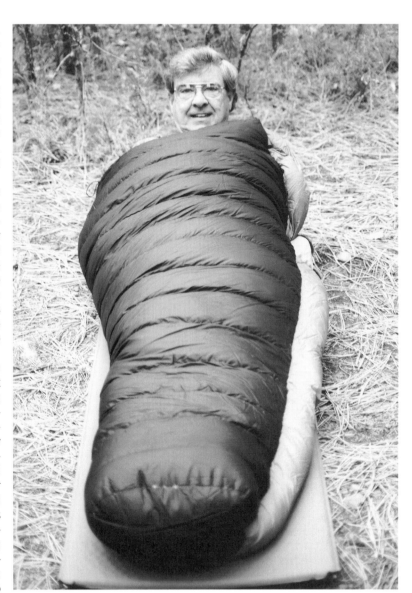

The efficient design of a mummy bag will keep you warm and cozy.

Bring a sleeping bag rated to the lowest temperature you plan to encounter. For treks into the desert or to very warm places, a summer bag rated to 40 or 50 degrees will be appropriate. For most backpacking trips, however, you'll want a bag that will keep you warm when the temperature drops in the evening. I tend to be a cold sleeper and won't go backpacking without a bag rated to at least 15 degrees. I also have a zero-degree bag that I use when I camp in colder climes. For the beginning backpacker, a bag rated to zero or below will probably be too warm. Keep in mind that the lower the temperature rating, the heavier and bulkier the bag will be.

The next decision you'll have to make is whether you want a sleeping bag filled with down or synthetic material. Traditionally, a good down fill has been considered warmer than a synthetic bag with the same temperature rating. This means that a 20-degree down bag will be a bit warmer than a 20-degree synthetic bag. A down bag will weigh less and stuff into a smaller sack than will a synthetic bag with a comparable rating. Today, however, many synthetic materials rival down bags in warmth and packability. A synthetic bag usually costs less (around $150, as compared with $200 for a down bag) and will keep you warmer should your bag get wet.

The bottom line is that it matters little what the bag is filled with. There are many affordable, quality bags constructed from both materials. Which material you choose will be a matter of personal preference. I have come to love the way down feels as it wraps around my body, so I prefer my down bag to my synthetic bag.

Before making a selection, also look at other features of the sleeping bag. Make sure the bag is long enough to accommodate your body, but avoid getting a bag that has a lot of extra room at your feet. Many manufacturers now make shorter bags for smaller people. If you are under 5 feet, 5 inches, consider buying a short bag. It will save weight and space in your pack, and it will keep you warmer.

Your sleeping bag should also have a drawcord that cinches the hood of the bag around your head. On cold nights, a snug collar on your bag will prevent warm air from escaping. Most sleeping bags have a two-way zipper so you can stick your feet out of the bottom of the bag on warm nights. A down bag should come with a large cotton storage sack.

No matter what type of bag you have, when you're on the trail, protect it from the elements by storing it in a durable, water-resistant stuff sack. In the morning your bag may be slightly damp from perspiration and condensation while you slept. It's a good idea to shake out the bag and let it air out before you pack it up. If it's a sunny morning, unzip your bag and drape it over a rock while you eat breakfast. Drying your sleeping bag will keep it performing as it should and will increase the life of the bag. (For more on cleaning and storing your sleeping bag, refer to appendix 4.)

Sleeping Mattress

Let's take a moment to clarify a misconception about camping: sleeping outside doesn't mean you have to spend the night tossing and turning on a rock-hard bed. Actually, sleeping outside can be quite cozy. Your sleeping bag will provide some cushion and insulation between you and the ground, but for a truly comfortable night's sleep, find yourself a decent sleeping mattress. I used to consider it a luxury; now I never go camping without one.

Again, you have some choices. There are two basic types of mattresses: inflatable mattresses and closed-cell foam pads.

Use an inflatable sleeping mattress for a sound sleep on any type of terrain.

Closed-cell foam pads are inexpensive ($20), lightweight, and virtually indestructible, but they are bulky and less comfortable than inflatable pads. I have a self-inflating pad ($55) that is considered three-quarter length (that is, it extends from my head to my knees). Mine is an inch thick and lightweight, and I wouldn't trade it for anything. If you're like me and opt for the more luxurious inflatable pad, consider bringing a patch kit in case your pad suffers a puncture wound.

Prices vary depending on the pad's thickness, length, and width. The best way to make a selection is to lie down in a sleeping bag on a sleeping pad. Is the pad long enough or is it too long? Will it provide enough insulation between you and the ground? How much does it weigh? When it's rolled up, does it fit in a small stuff sack? Choose a mattress that feels right to you. (Cleaning and storage techniques for your mattress can be found in appendix 4.)

Pillow

Yes, you can have a pillow when you camp—there's no need to deny yourself the comforts of home. You just won't be lugging along the pillow that's on your bed. Stuff some cozy clothes in the hood of your sleeping bag and tighten the drawstring on the hood to keep them in place. I like to use a soft fleece jacket as a pillow. Or, make a pillow by filling a stuff sack with clothes you won't be wearing to bed.

OTHER BACKPACKING GEAR

In addition to a first-aid kit and a personal hygiene kit, which we'll discuss later in this book (information on first aid is found on pages 78 to 80 and 83 to 85, and personal hygiene is discussed on pages 74 to 77), you'll likely fill the rest of your pack with odds and ends. Whether you take many of the smaller items will depend on when and where you'll be traveling. It will also depend on your interests and on your physical condition. Some people will need to bring contact lenses and saline solution, special medication, or a bee-sting kit. I've met people who insist on filling the extra space in their packs with knickknacks so they can decorate the interior of the tent. For most of us, weight will be a limiting factor, and we'll take only the items that we'll use every day.

Although much of the gear mentioned in this section is optional, two items that I recommend you take on every trip are a light and a knife.

Light

It's nice to have a light when you need to answer nature's call in the middle of the night, when you crawl out of the tent in the dark to secure the rainfly, or when you're trying to locate your gloves after the sun has gone down. You probably won't plan on hiking at night, but at least once in your backpacking career you will probably find yourself tromping along a trail in the dark, searching for a campsite; it's best to be prepared should you find yourself in that situation.

When you backpack, carry a tiny flashlight or a headlamp. Small flashlights are inexpensive, weigh very little, and are easy to store in your pack—I keep mine in the top pouch of my backpack. Many hikers prefer to use a headlamp because it frees up their hands. It's much easier to pitch a tent at night when you're wearing a head-

A headlamp.

lamp than it is when you're trying to hang on to a flashlight! Either way, carry something that will light your way, and make sure the batteries in your flashlight or headlamp are fresh. On longer trips you may want to bring spare batteries.

Knife

It is also a good idea to carry a knife. You may need to cut food, bandages in your first-aid kit, or patches in your repair kit. Some hikers feel more secure knowing they are carrying some sort of weapon, although I have yet to meet a backpacker who actually used a knife for self-defense. Still, you never know when a knife will come in handy.

When choosing a knife, think about the size and weight of the blade. For basic backpacking trips, you don't need to sport an 8-inch blade on your hipbelt. Think about what you'll use the

knife for. If you'll use it to spread peanut butter and cut moleskin, a large blade will be unnecessary. I primarily use a knife to slice cheese, and for most trips I've found that a tiny pocket knife serves all my cutting needs.

"Great-to-Have" Items

You will need to be prepared in the unfortunate event that your gear should break. It's not unlikely that sometime during your travels your sleeping mattress will suffer a puncture wound or a pack strap will rip loose. To avoid an unpleasant night or a shortened trip, I toss a couple of items into a resealable plastic bag and call it a repair kit. I bring a couple of patches in case my sleeping mattress springs a leak. I use patches or ripstop nylon tape to repair tears in my tent, sleeping bag, and backpack. I bring an extra shoelace or a length of para-

Using an umbrella may be the best way to stay dry. But be careful on those windy ridges!

chute cord to replace a broken boot lace. A couple of heavy-duty safety pins and a needle and thread will come in handy if you get in a bind. Assemble your repair kit and store it in your backpack—that way, you'll never leave home without it. Somewhere down the trail, when a piece of equipment breaks, congratulate yourself for bringing the items you need to fix it.

Depending on where you're going, you may want to bring with you a few other items. When I arrive at my destination for the night, the first thing I do is change into my camp clothes—something cotton and cozy. I also like to retire the hiking boots for the evening and slip on a pair of camp shoes. I prefer sandals. Some people prefer sneakers. On colder trips, a pair of down booties is luxurious!

For steep ascents and descents, a pair of trekking poles will come in handy. Many trekking poles are equipped with an internal spring or a synthetic gel that acts as a shock absorber. Most models are telescoping, which means they shrink down to about 2 feet. This makes it easy to strap the poles to your backpack when you don't need them. Higher-end models have a compass or a camera mount built in to the pole grip, and some can be converted into an avalanche probe.

Trekking poles can be expensive ($90), so if you're working within a tight budget, try using an old pair of ski poles or a hiking stick. Any type of pole will give your legs a break and make the climb a little easier. One pole is better than none, but two poles will keep your body balanced and take an equal amount of weight off both legs.

When traveling in bear country, you may want to bring pepper spray. If there's a chance you'll be sharing your experience with mosquitoes, bring bug repellent or a mesh head net. Use parachute cord to hang your food at night, no matter whose habitat you're passing through (proper food storage techniques are discussed on pages 72 to 73).

Other items to add to your pack include sunglasses, a book, journal, writing implement, personal identification, and a camera. A watch will help you determine your pace and how many hours of daylight you have left. And, of course, don't forget the umbrella! (See appendix 2 for an equipment checklist.)

THE BACKPACKER'S KITCHEN

The four components to the backpacker's kitchen, each of which plays a role in maintaining good health and providing you with the energy you need to backpack, are nutritious food, water and the devices used to make it potable, a stove, and cookware.

FOOD

You won't be able to change your menu halfway to your destination, so it's important to make good choices when you select food for a trip. Food selection is a fun part of the planning process because it forces you to be creative and pay close attention to detail. I really enjoy menu planning; I envision the trip and imagine what foods my body will be craving. It's a tricky balance to bring enough food to keep you happily hiking but not too much that your pack weighs 50 pounds. As you plan your menu, consider weight, calories, nutrition, and packability.

Weight

At first it may seem challenging to find foods that are lightweight. Items such as fruit, soda, canned soup, and a container of lasagna are not worth their weight when they have to be lugged up a mountain. The trick is to bring dehydrated foods— that is, foods that no longer contain water. Dehydrated food retains its prior nutritional value, has the same number of calories, and comes back to life when you add water. This way, you can carry lightweight food and add the weight of water once you're happily resting at camp.

You'll find many dehydrated foods at your local grocer: dried apricots, dried pineapple, raisins, beef or turkey jerky, and soup mixes. Foods such as pasta, instant rice, instant mashed potatoes, and oatmeal are lightweight and easy to prepare. Add flavoring packets to pasta and rice. Cheese and spices add pizzazz to almost anything. You can find food preparation ideas from a number of books on backcountry cuisine. (Refer to the books listed in

A food dehydrator.

appendix 5.) The food selections you make will depend on your style. Some backpackers prefer to eat macaroni and cheese and oatmeal every day; others spend hours preparing gourmet meals.

Some hikers buy prepackaged, freeze-dried meals that are sold at outfitting stores. A dinner will typically cost about $7, which is a bit expensive for my backcountry budget, but the person who shows up at camp with chicken and vegetable Thai curry or beef Stroganoff is the envy of everyone. Most freeze-dried selections are quite tasty, and they are easy to prepare. Add boiling water, stir, let it sit for 10 minutes, and your dinner is ready to eat!

For most of us, though, the freeze-dried selections will be a rare treat, so we ought to spend some time talking about alternatives. A great way to get tasty meals in the backcountry is to dehydrate your own home-cooked concoctions. Food dehydrators can cost as little as $30, and they can be purchased at any appliance or department store. They allow you to turn pasta sauce into powder, reduce pounds of vegetables and beans to ounces, dry your own fruit and jerky, and best of all, dehydrate your favorite soups, stews, and stir fries. A dehydrator consists of a stack of trays through which warm air is blown to dry out the food. Every spring I spend a few days dehydrating home-cooked meals for the backpacking season. I dry fruit like apples, apricots, and pineapple; vegetables like mushrooms, corn, peas, and potatoes; beef; and black bean soup, chicken and vegetable stir fries, and turkey chili.

When you dehydrate your own food, note the amount of hydrated food you put on each tray. For example, I can put two dinners of black bean soup on one tray. When the soup is dried, I know that the cup of powder, even though it looks like very little, is enough for two dinners. I put the powder into a resealable freezer bag and label the bag with the contents and the amount. When you arrive at camp, boil water and stir in your dehydrated meal. You will have to experiment with how much water is required to rehydrate certain foods. Also, some foods like meat, potatoes, and beans take longer to come back to life. I usually let my dinner soak in hot water for a half hour, then boil it again for a few minutes before I indulge.

Calories

Some hikers do elaborate calorie counts to determine precisely how much food they need for a three-day backpacking trip. Most people, including me, prefer to bring the same amount of food they normally eat in a day, then throw in a bunch of snacks. Remember, it is important to have enough food to keep you going, but it is equally important to be carrying only what you need. If you overestimate your appetite and end up lugging an extra 10 pounds of food for four days, I guarantee you will plan better next time.

Nutrition

A backpacking trip is not the time to starve yourself, and it is not the time to go on a sugar binge. Yes, you absolutely deserve the foods you love, and you deserve a treat at the end of the day, but eating candy bars all day will get you only so far. Plan a balanced diet, one that consists of carbohydrates, proteins, and fats in a 50:25:25 ratio. That means that 50 percent of your diet should be composed of carbohydrates, such as those found in breads and grains. Twenty-five percent of your diet should be protein, found in foods like nuts, meats, and beans. And 25 percent should be composed of fat.

Hikers usually don't have a problem getting enough carbohydrates on a backpacking trip because the simplest meals to prepare—pasta and rice dishes, for example—are loaded with carbohydrates. Snacks such as energy bars, cereal, chips and crackers, and trail mixes are also high in carbohydrates. Another way to get a little extra energy is to add powdered sports drink mixes to your water jug.

Protein is a little more difficult to incorporate, but it is essential for building and maintaining muscle. Try lentils, bean dishes, jerky, and nuts. Find energy bars that are high in protein, or add one of the many protein shake mixes to your water.

Fat is present in many of the foods that are high in protein, and in general, we don't seem to have a problem getting enough fat into our diets. Sometimes, however, men who are very fit have a difficult time maintaining their weight on backpacking trips, so they need to eat a higher amount of fat. To make sure they get enough, some hikers like to add a chunk of butter to their backcountry dinners to make the meal stick to their bones.

Give some thought to the food that is going to fuel your body on your trip. If you give your body the food it needs, you will have boundless energy and be able to travel more easily to your destination.

Still wondering what to bring? Try these menu suggestions. For breakfast, consider cereal with dehydrated milk, toaster pastries, oatmeal, grits, cream of wheat, dried fruit, and nuts. Some hikers cook omelets or pancakes and sausage. Throughout the day, snack on trail mix, energy bars, granola, nuts, dried fruit, corn chips, peanut butter crackers, and jerky. For prepared meals, consider pasta with cheese sauces or a variety of red or white sauces. Add dehydrated vegetables and a tin of chicken to pasta or rice. Try your favorite home-cooked soups or stews, hummus and pita bread, tabouli, couscous, rice and beans, instant soups, instant refried beans, and stir-fries with chicken, beef, or tofu.

I always put a few tea bags in a resealable plastic bag as well. Some people prefer instant coffee bags or packets of hot chocolate or cider. Whatever your preference, a hot mug of something is quite a treat on a cool morning or after you've arrived at camp. And chocolate is always my treat of choice.

Packability

As you plan your menu, think about bringing foods that are dense. You need to be able to store a lot of food in a very small space, so you don't want to fill your entire backpack with rice cakes or marshmallows. Food such as beans, cheese, and peanut butter are packed with energy and take up little room in your pack.

Also select food that won't spoil. Dehydrated selections are especially good. Cheese, fruit, butter, and other dairy products and produce will last a few days, but leave the turkey sandwich at home unless you plan to eat it that day.

Food Tips for the Trail

I admit, culinary skills are not my strong point. I used to think of dinner as a series of snacks that could be eaten while hovering over the kitchen sink, and except for major holidays, the oven was ignored. I was the person who made a daily trip to the supermarket because I lived meal to meal. So when I realized that I had to plan food for a backpacking trip for an entire week, I was terrified.

I made a lot of mistakes with food on my first few backpacking trips. Scared that I wouldn't have enough food, I carried way too much. I allowed myself double what I was used to eating at home, figuring that I would be starving out there in the woods. I later realized that average-sized meals can be supplemented with a few snacks to satisfy the backpacker's appetite.

Unaccustomed to menu planning, I arranged to eat the same food items over and over: oatmeal for breakfast, peanut butter sandwiches for lunch, pasta for dinner. No matter how much you like peanut butter and jelly, after a few days it gets old. On my six-month Appalachian Trail hike, I got so tired of oatmeal, instant mashed potatoes, and instant rice that I began eating only candy bars, toaster pastries, and an occasional meal of pasta.

Since then I've come a long way. I learned that when I eat a balanced diet on the trail, I feel better. I am able to cover more ground and feel strong doing it. When I am fueled with nutritious food, I seem to have the mental stamina to deal more gracefully with inclement weather, mosquitoes, and misleading trail signs. Cutting back on junk food snacks like candy bars, sweet cereals, and energy bars that are high in sugar has made me feel better on the trail and has helped me sleep more soundly.

Diversifying food selections is key. I do this by preparing meals at home and dehydrating them in a food dehydrator. On the trail I alternate store-bought meals like beans and rice with home-cooked stews and chili. On every trip I carry a variety of dried fruit, different kinds of nuts, different types of jerky, and various kinds of cheese and crackers. Now I look forward to dinner after a long day of hiking, and it's far more enjoyable to hover over a camp stove, stirring spices into a steaming pot and chatting with friends, than it is to eat peanut butter crackers over the kitchen sink!

raisins

macaroni

potato soup mix

energy bar

powered cheese sauce

dried pineapple

powdered sports drink

cereal

tea bags

Lightweight, calorie-dense, easy-to-prepare foods are best for backpacking.

Whichever foods you've selected for your trip, you will want to repackage most of them. As I mentioned in Backpacking 101, you don't need to bring the entire hunk of cheese and a big box of crackers. You also don't need the entire 5-pound bag of pasta and the entire jar of peanut butter. Bring only the amount you will eat. Place the amount of food you need in a resealable freezer bag or in a small plastic jar. This way your food will stay dry and clean, and you can reseal the bag or jar.

If you want to bring items that are easily crushed, like crackers or bread, consider putting them in a tennis ball can, or learn to live with crushed crackers. You may also want to put pinches of spices in tiny plastic bags or in film containers.

Most of my food goes in one stuff sack. The items I'm likely to eat first go in last. I keep snacks for the day in an external pocket or in the top pouch of my backpack so I don't need to dig through my pack every time I want a snack.

WATER

In hot, dry areas, or along trails that are far from water, you may have to carry a lot of water with you. On most backpacking trips, however, a 1-quart jug of water and a bladder bag will suffice. A bladder bag is a larger sack that can be used to collect water once you get to camp. Filling a large bladder bag prevents you from having to make several trips to the water source.

It's usually not possible or practical to carry with you all the water you need for a backpacking trip, so you will need to plan your trip around water and have a way to make potable the water that you come across. You will need water for drinking, preparing your meals, bathing, brushing, and washing dishes and clothes. It is convenient to camp near a lake or stream, and it is nice to be relatively close to water at various times throughout the day. Look at a map of the area to determine how close the trail is to various water sources.

Consider the time of the year and previous weather conditions. Check with a ranger to see whether streams are running, springs are flowing, and campsites have water close by.

Thirty years ago, many hikers drank directly from streams. I wish we were able to do that today, but unfortunately many of our water sources are polluted from industry and agriculture, and many sources contain microscopic viruses, bacteria, organic chemicals, or parasites that are harmful to us. There is no way to determine whether a source is safe by looking at it, no matter how clear it looks, which is why it is best to treat all water as if it contains something harmful. There are three ways to treat water: boiling, chemical treatment, and filtration.

Boiling

Bringing water to a roiling boil will kill everything in it, but boiling is inefficient because it takes a lot of time and fuel, and you have to let the water cool before you can drink it.

The only time I prefer boiling as a treatment method is when I'm established at camp and am preparing dinner or making tea. You can take water right from the source, boil it, then add your pasta or pour it in a mug for tea.

Chemical Treatment

A chemical treatment like iodine is a good alternative to boiling. A bottle of iodine tablets is inexpensive ($7) and weighs almost nothing, but you should wait about twenty minutes after adding the tablets to the water before you drink it. Some people don't like the taste of chemically treated water. To alter the taste, try adding a flavored drink mix.

Iodine will protect you against protozoans, bacteria, and viruses, but it will not kill a protozoan called *Cryptosporidium*. This critter is pretty rare and most hikers are willing to take the chance; but

At camp or on the trail, use a bladder bag to transport water.

if you're concerned about *Cryptosporidium*, you may want to use a different method of treatment. Also, if you are pregnant or nursing, or have thyroid or goiter problems, consult a physician before using iodine.

Filtration

There are a number of advantages to using a water filter. In addition to removing harmful microorganisms, filters remove visible particles like chunks of leaves and bugs. They are fairly easy to use, and you can drink the filtered water immediately. A water filter can cost anywhere from $30 to $300, depending on its capabilities and design.

Understand that there is a difference between filters and purifiers: *water filters* strain water through pores, and the effectiveness of the filter depends on the pore size (smaller pores will filter out more microorganisms); *purifiers* are filters that use chemical treatments to get rid of viruses, heavy metals, herbicides, and pesticides. Purifiers are typically at the higher end of the price range.

On either a filter or a purifier, the actual filter cartridge will need to be cleaned or replaced on a regular basis. To make the filter last longer, avoid filtering visibly dirty water. If you must use your filter in a mucky pond, put a coffee filter over the intake hose. Don't let the intake hose rest on the lake or stream bottom. If water appears very silty, put untreated water in a pot to let the silt settle out before you filter it. You may also want to periodically flush the filter with bleach to prevent microorganisms from multiplying while your filter is being stored for long periods. (Cleaning and storage techniques are found in appendix 4.)

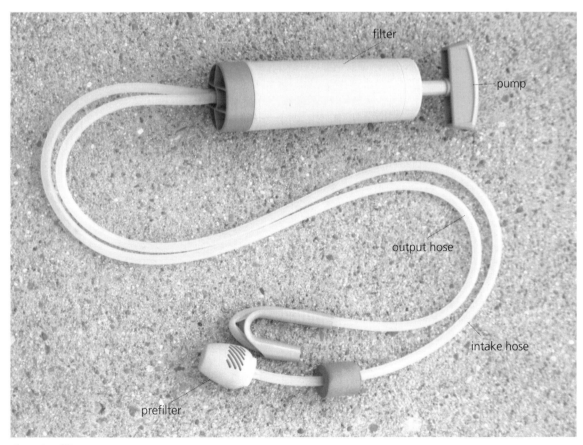

A water filter.

Filter water to avoid ingesting harmful microorganisms.

STOVES

Some backpackers practice minimum-weight traveling; they eat only cold food so they don't have to carry a stove and fuel. For those of us who like a hot meal, however, single-burner camp stoves are the preferred method of cooking.

If you're in the market for a stove, consider the following: Do you need a three-season stove or one that works in the winter as well? Will you be cooking at high altitudes? Consider how much the stove weighs and how long the stove takes to boil water.

What kind of fuel do you prefer to use: propane, butane, auto gas, kerosene, alcohol, or white gas? This is the big question, and the one that will likely determine which stove you choose. Stoves fall into two categories: those that burn butane and propane canisters and those that burn liquid fuel. Manufacturers are beginning to make stoves that burn both canisters and liquid fuel, and many stoves that burn liquid fuel can burn *any* of the liquid fuels (auto gas, kerosene, alcohol, or white gas). Still, you will need to decide which type of fuel you prefer to burn.

White gas, also known as Coleman fuel, is the preferred fuel (especially on longer trips or winter trips) because it is inexpensive, it burns clean, and it's sold at outfitting stores, hardware stores, and some supermarkets. Kerosene can be found in any country, but it's more difficult to light and has a tendency to clog fuel lines. Denatured alcohol provides the cleanest burn, but the fuel is often expensive and

Backcountry Improv

My partner and I were on the eighteenth day of a thirty-four-day hike along the Colorado Trail when our stove broke. It was cool and breezy as we ascended grassy alpine summits, wound through aspen groves, and forded icy streams. By mile 15, I was having visions of a piping hot pasta dinner. After a day of snacking, we deserved a meal with substance. That evening we found a grassy ledge above a river and sprawled out our gear. My partner went to the river to fetch water for cooking, and I removed the stove and fuel bottle from my backpack. As I reached for the fuel bottle, I did a double take. Something was missing. To my horror, the pump on the fuel bottle had snapped off.

Gone. And with no pump, there was no hot pasta. As my partner trudged up the hill to camp, I had to deliver the bad news: dinner would now consist of cold couscous. I don't know if we were more upset because we had to eat cold food or because we weight-conscious backpackers had to lug around a stove and full fuel bottle that were now useless.

I had been carrying the fuel bottle in a pocket on the outside of my backpack. During one of our rest breaks, I must have smacked the pack against a rock, which broke the fuel pump. We suffered through a cold dinner and headed to town the next day. After a few conversations with employees at outfitting stores and hardware stores, we learned that the part would have to be ordered, which could take up to a week. Eager to get back to the trail, we chose to abandon the stove and make a new one. We emptied a small tuna fish can, cut slits around the sides, and purchased a small bottle of rubbing alcohol. At night we would fill the bottom of the tuna can with alcohol, light it, and place a small pot of water over the flame. It took twenty to thirty minutes to heat our food, as compared with five to ten minutes with a camp stove, but we were able to enjoy hot dinners for the remainder of the trip, and we relished having a stove that weighed almost nothing.

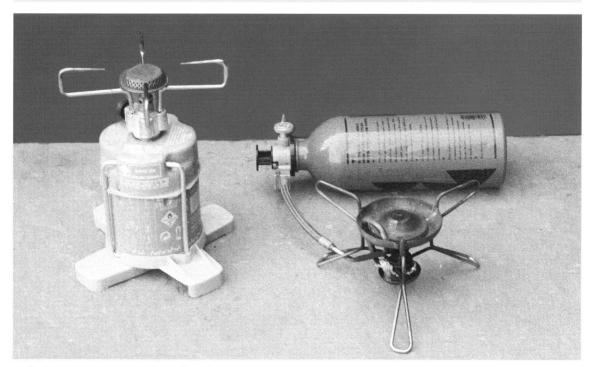

Left: A canister stove. Right: a liquid-fuel stove.

fuel line

fuel valve

fuel canister

flame

stove legs provide stability

This stove can use both canisters and liquid fuel.

difficult to find in remote places. Automotive gas is a filthy fuel; it will coat your stove and pot with soot, but it's cheap and easy to find. If you're in a bind, use the lowest octane unleaded available.

Propane and butane canister stoves are favored by many backpackers because they tend to be quiet, convenient, easy to operate, and inexpensive (around $30, compared with $60 for a liquid-fuel stove). Unfortunately, most canisters must be thrown out after they have been used, which seems to create a lot of unnecessary waste. The right type of canister may also be difficult to find if you're far from home, and replacement fuel canisters cost more than an equivalent amount of most liquid fuels. Canister stoves have also been known to be finicky in cold weather.

Whichever model you select, light the stove before you buy it. At first you may not feel comfortable lighting the stove, and that's OK. Ask a salesperson to show you how to light it and practice with an experienced friend or salesperson. After you light it a couple of times, it will be much less intimidating. (For information on cleaning and storing your stove, refer to appendix 4.)

COOKWARE

Pay attention to weight and durability when you're selecting cookware. To keep your pack weight down, choose cookware that is constructed from aluminum, stainless steel, titanium, or a combination of these materials. Aluminum is the lightest and least expensive, but it is the least durable. Stainless steel is a good choice because it's more durable than aluminum, and titanium is likely the best choice if your budget can afford it.

The easiest way to cut weight with cookware is to leave most of it at home. I carry one 2-quart pot, a lid, a spoon, and a mug. That's it. If you prepare extravagant, multicourse meals, you may need additional pots. If you travel with a group, bring one large pot and aluminum or plastic bowls for each person.

I can eat everything I bring with a spoon, so I leave the fork at home. Be wary of plastic utensils from fast-food restaurants; they break easily. Silverware is heavy to lug through the backcountry, so your best bet is a spoon made of Lexan. You'll find one at your local outfitting store.

COOKING TIPS

The following cooking tips may come in handy when preparing meals in the backcountry:

- Disassemble your stove at home to get a feel for how it works. This will make it easier to repair or clean the stove in the field.
- Practice lighting the stove at home until you feel comfortable with it. In the field, experiment with the pressure (on a liquid-fuel stove) and adjust the fuel valve (on either type of stove) to make the stove simmer and boil. Each stove requires a different touch. With a little practice, you will have water boiling, simmering, or warming slowly.
- Paint the outside of your cookware with black, heat-resistant paint; this will decrease boiling time.
- Never transport fuel on an airplane. To make your fuel bottle safe for air travel, expose the empty fuel bottle to the sun for a couple hours. Then pack it up.
- As a general guideline, for three-season trekking at low elevations, bring 5 ounces of white gas per couple per day, or 125 grams of canister fuel per couple per day.
- Water takes longer to boil at high elevations or in lower tem-

peratures, so plan to bring more fuel when traveling in these conditions.
- In addition to a lighter, bring waterproof matches as a backup.
- Use a stove-pricker (if one didn't come with your stove, you can buy one at an outdoor outfitter) to clean the fuel line on your stove periodically, unless your stove is self-cleaning.
- A windscreen will shield the stove from wind and increase boiling time.
- Cover the pot with a lid when you're boiling water.
- Never use a stove inside a tent. Tent material is highly flammable, and carbon monoxide from your stove can kill you if there's no ventilation.
- Keep clothing and gear away from the stove, especially when you're lighting it.
- Store the fuel container in an exterior pocket of your backpack, and keep it away from your food in case it leaks.

Basic cookware: pot with lid, spoon, mug.

SKILLS AND TECHNIQUES

There are a number of preparations you can make and skills you can learn long before you set foot in the woods. The amount of time and energy you devote to backcountry preparations is up to you. You may want to begin improving your fitness three months before your trip, or you may elect to start training three weeks before you go. Some beginners may take a map and compass course months ahead of time and practice route finding before their trip. Some hikers like to assemble their gear a week before they depart. Others seal the seams on their tent and waterproof their boots the night before. It is possible to throw together a trip at the last minute, but recognize that you will likely have a safer, more comfortable journey if you take time to prepare and familiarize yourself with a few basic skills and techniques before you head into the backcountry.

FITNESS

People often ask me if you have to be in great physical shape to backpack. The answer, quite frankly, is no, but it helps. Anyone who can walk can backpack. You don't need to be able to run the Boston Marathon or climb Mount Everest. I have seen people backpack who hadn't seriously exercised in months. I've seen smokers backpack, and I've seen very overweight people backpack. Those people will be the first to admit, however, that it was a challenge. The simple truth is this: the better physical condition you're in, the easier backpacking will be.

If you know you will be going on a backpacking trip soon, there are a few things you can do to improve your fitness. If you are not in the habit of exercising, consult a personal trainer at your local health club. If you're on a program, continue to do it, and make sure it involves the following components: endurance training, strength training, and flexibility. That means that you should be doing something like jogging or biking that gets your heart rate up, you should be lifting weights, and you should be stretching.

Exercises like abdominal crunches and calf raises can be done in the gym or at your house;

Lunges will strengthen your legs for backpacking. In lunge position, make sure your knee does not extend past your ankle.

they strengthen muscles that will help propel your body up the mountains. When doing abdominal crunches, lie on your back with your knees bent, clasp your hands behind your head, and move your chest toward your knees. Work slowly so you feel your abdominals engaging, and remember to breathe. For calf raises, stand on a step and let your heels hang off. Come up onto the balls of your feet, hold for a second, then let your heels drop below the step. Work slowly and stretch your calves after performing the exercise. A personal trainer can recommend many exercises to strengthen your

Climbing stadium steps will improve your ability to traverse mountainous terrain.

backpacking muscles; but I've found that the best way to simulate backpacking without setting foot on a trail is to do lunges or climb stadium steps with a loaded backpack.

When you do lunges, make sure your front knee is directly above your ankle. Be careful not to extend your knee beyond that point. Start out with an empty pack and add weight incrementally as your fitness improves. I like to add weight to my pack by filling it with backpacking gear. Whatever you use, make sure the weight is evenly distributed throughout the pack; avoid weighting the pack with things like books and barbells that will concentrate all the weight at the bottom of the pack.

After your workout and after every day hike, remember to stretch. Devote as much time as you can to stretching and be sure to hit the large muscle groups in your legs: quadriceps, hamstrings, and calves. Hold each stretch for about thirty seconds. Stretching will not only make you feel better the next day, but it will help prevent injuries, in the gym and on the trail.

A good fitness program will no doubt make you a healthier person, but the best way to train specifically for backpacking is to go backpacking. When I train for longer excursions I continue to do my regular strength training and stretching routines at the gym, but I do all my endurance training outside. I hike the trails near my home with a loaded backpack. It gets my legs accustomed to climbing hills and walking on uneven terrain. Trust me, stair-climbing machines can simulate only so much!

STAYING DRY

Your efforts to stay dry in the backcountry should start at home. Start by treating your hiking boots with a water-repellency treatment (as discussed on pages 25 to 26). Most rain pants and rainjackets can also be treated to enhance and maintain their water-repellent qualities. I use a treatment for my Gore-Tex jacket that can be poured into the washing machine. After one wash cycle, water beads up on my jacket as if it were brand-new. Your salesperson can direct you to the treatment that is appropriate for your garments.

Of course, you want your shelter to be waterproof, too. Ensure that it will be by sealing the seams on your tent and rainfly. If your tent doesn't come with a small tube of seam sealer, purchase one from your outfitting store. Choose a clear, sunny day and erect your tent outside. Crawl inside the tent and apply the seam sealer to the seams around the floor of the tent. Then attach the rainfly to the tent, but put it on inside out. Apply seam sealer to all the seams on the fly. Allow sufficient time for the seam sealer to dry before you pack up the tent.

PACKING THE PACK

How you organize your gear depends largely on the type of backpack (internal or external frame) you use. You will soon develop an organization system that works well for you and your pack. If you use an internal-frame pack, most of your gear will be stored inside the main compartment. This system protects your gear from the elements but makes it more difficult to locate particular items. Organizing gear is easier in external-frame packs, but items outside the pack will likely see more wear

and tear. As you begin to pack your gear, think about where the weight will be distributed. Most backpackers like the heaviest items close to their bodies. To maintain a lower center of gravity and better stability, put heavier items toward the bottom of the pack. Some people find it more comfortable on gentle terrain to carry heavier items in the top part of the pack. Experiment to see what feels right to you.

When using an interior-frame backpack, I always put my sleeping bag in the bottom of the pack. On top of the sleeping bag I store clothing, my bivy bag, my sleeping mattress, and food that I won't be eating that day. The stove, cookware, and personal items go on top, and the fuel bottle and water bottle go in pockets outside the pack. In the top pouch, I keep snacks and personal items like lip balm, bug repellent, iodine tablets, and a first-aid kit. Keep items that you may need to access quickly in the top pouch or in other easy-to-get-to places.

When using an external-frame backpack, I strap the tent to the frame below the main compartment and sometimes strap a sleeping mattress to the top of the pack. My sleeping bag goes in the bottom of the main compartment. I fill the interior with larger items like cookware, food, and

Late-Night Leaks

Too often I've awakened in the middle of the night with wet toes and pools of water in the corners of the tent. Once the water is in, there is not a lot you can do about it. I imagine a conscientious backpacker would trudge out into the night to adjust the tent's rainfly or at least try to figure out how the water is entering. In my little world, at 2 A.M. on a dark, rainy night, it never occurs to me to do anything besides scoot toward the dry spot and will myself back to sleep.

There was one night, however, when there was no way to go back to sleep. My friend and I were experimenting with a tarp and apparently did an insufficient job rigging

it. Heavy rains fell throughout the night and the tarp eventually became waterlogged and sagged toward the ground. I woke every hour or so to find the material an inch or two closer to my head. I woke one final time when the wet material touched my face and began funneling a stream of water onto my sleeping bag. That night there was some groaning and cursing and the muttering of phrases like, "Never again."

I've learned that it's difficult to get dry in the field once you get wet. It's far easier and more comfortable to plan for rain before you leave for a backpacking trip than it is to get dry in the middle of the

night in the middle of nowhere. I now seam seal a tent as soon as I get it. I treat my boots with a water-repellency product and reapply it every few weeks. I store all my gear in waterproof or water-resistant stuff sacks, and I bring a good rainjacket or umbrella on all trips.

No matter how tired I am at the end of the day, I take time to choose a campsite that won't collect water and to properly secure the tent's rainfly or to string a tarp so the material is taut and secure. There's nothing more reassuring than hearing the ping of raindrops as they are deflected from the tent. Then you can lie back and mutter things like, "Bring it on!"

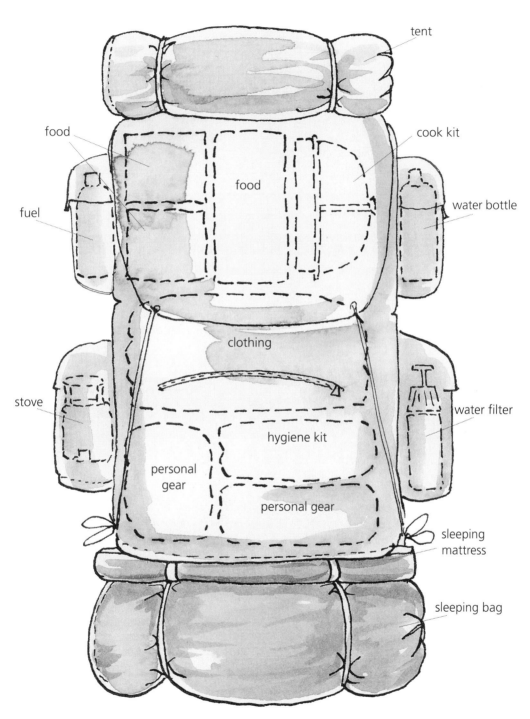

tent

food

cook kit

fuel

water bottle

food

clothing

stove

water filter

hygiene kit

personal gear

personal gear

sleeping mattress

sleeping bag

One option for organizing gear in your pack.

clothing, and I relegate smaller items like sandals, my hygiene kit, and water purification to external pockets. Make sure personal items and snacks are easy to access, and always store fuel and water outside the main compartment.

In any case, make sure your pack fly and a rain-jacket are easily accessible. A rainstorm can come out of nowhere, and you don't want to be turning your pack inside out trying to locate a jacket in the middle of a downpour. To keep contents of your pack dry, pack everything—especially a camera, journal, and other personal items—in resealable plastic bags. Larger items like your food and clothes can be put in differently colored stuff sacks. When you need something, you ought to know just where to find it.

Your loaded backpack should weigh no more than one-fourth of your body weight. On very long trips, trips in cold weather, or trips in places where you need to carry lots of water, your pack may weigh a bit more. Strive to carry the lightest weight possible—that's the best way to make the walking easier.

PUTTING ON THE PACK

To mount your loaded backpack without straining yourself, follow this procedure. Start by loosening all the straps on the pack. With the harness facing you, hold on to the pack as it rests on the ground. With bent knees and a straight back, lift the pack to your thigh. Slip your right arm through one shoulder strap and swing the pack onto your right shoulder. Put your left arm through the other shoulder strap. Clasp and tighten the hipbelt, tighten the shoulder straps, and then adjust the load lifter straps and the sternum strap. You're ready to go!

If you cannot lift the pack comfortably, then you may have overpacked. Get rid of gear that is not essential, or take smaller versions of necessary items. If you won't part with any of the packed items, get someone to help you put the pack on so you don't strain your back. Have your partner stand behind you and hold the pack up (as if you were going to put on a coat) while you slip your

Putting on the backpack: 1. Bend your knees and grab the shoulder straps. 2. Lift the pack and rest it on your thigh.

3. Put your right arm through the shoulder strap. 4. Straighten your legs, swing the pack onto your back, and slip your left arm through the other shoulder strap. 5. Make sure both shoulder straps are seated properly. 6. Clasp and tighten the hipbelt.

Cutting Ounces

When I started hiking the Appalachian Trail, I struggled beneath a 45-pound backpack, and my partner shouldered a 65-pound load. After the first few grueling climbs, we knew that we would never make it unless we learned to lighten our packs. We began sending extra food and gear home. Every ounce counted. We got rid of bowls and cooking utensils. We carried only one pot and two spoons.

Most backpackers seem to carry too many toiletries, and although they are usually small items, they add up. I reduced the contents of my toiletry bag by half, getting rid of anything that wasn't necessary for survival or imperative for my personal comfort. I sent home a watch, a second T-shirt, deodorant, and extra hair ties, and I carried only the tiniest tubes of toothpaste, suntan lotion, and bug repellent. We cut our toothbrushes in half, sent home the books and cards, and by the end of the trail, my loaded backpack weighed between 25 and 30 pounds, and my partner's was down to 30 to 35.

After we began to lighten our loads, it quickly became apparent that we didn't miss anything we had sent back. The pleasure of the experience was provided by the surroundings and by our attitudes. If we were uncomfortable or unhappy, it was never because of some piece of gear that we wished we had.

arms through the shoulder straps. Your partner should support the weight until you've clasped the hipbelt and secured the load on your back.

MAP AND COMPASS

Map Skills

As a backpacker, you ought to be familiar with two types of maps: planimetric and topographic. Planimetric maps show the features of the land. Use planimetric maps to get a general feel for the area and to determine how to access trailheads. When you're on a trip, however, you'll want to use a topographic map (or topo map). A topo map shows how the ground is shaped; contour lines on the map connect areas of similar elevation so you can determine how many feet you will need to ascend to get to your campsite and how steep the terrain will be. Your map will include a scale that will give you the distance that is represented between each contour line. For example, on many topo maps, the distance between contour lines represents 200 feet. If the map shows your trail passing through five contour lines, you know you will be climbing or descending 1,000 feet in elevation.

Contour lines that are far apart represent gentle terrain, while lines that are close together indicate a very steep slope. When a trail follows a contour line, you know you'll be walking on relatively flat terrain. If the map shows a trail that is perpendicular to a series of contour lines, the trail is going straight up the mountain. By studying the topo map, you can plan a route that suits your abilities. If the trip is already planned, you can at least mentally prepare yourself for what lies ahead.

One word of caution. Sometimes you'll find trail maps at trailheads, ranger stations, or tourist centers. They show crude representations of natural features and are often not drawn to scale. Using a compass with this type of map is often a futile effort. If the trail is short and well marked, or if you're familiar with the route, you may not feel the need to carry a more detailed map. But keep in mind that emergency situations can arise anywhere, so it's best to navigate even the most familiar territory with a detailed topographic map (map resources are listed in appendix 5).

Before you leave, use the map to estimate distances. Determine how many miles you will cover each day, and determine how far apart water sources are. Water sources are usually colored in blue. A creek or a spring that does not flow year-round may be represented by a dashed blue line instead of a solid line.

As you walk, notice your surroundings. Make a mental note of things you pass (a meadow, a trail junction, a narrow canyon). Keep track of the rivers you cross, the passes you climb, and directional

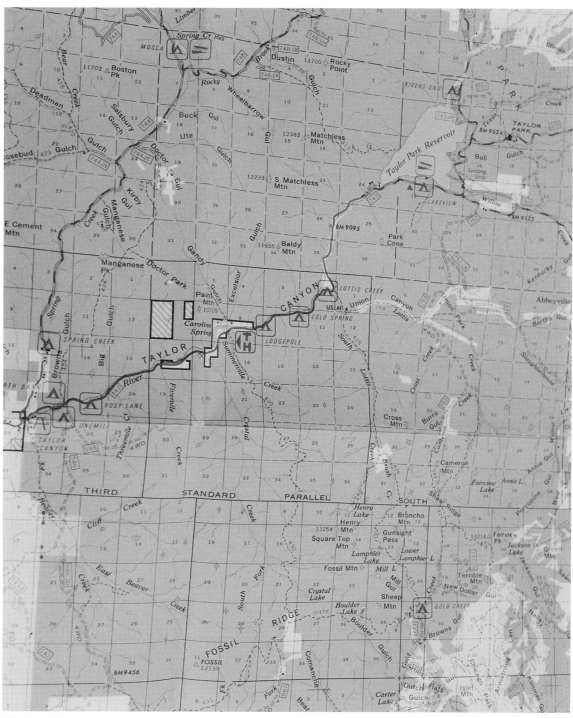

Planimetric map.

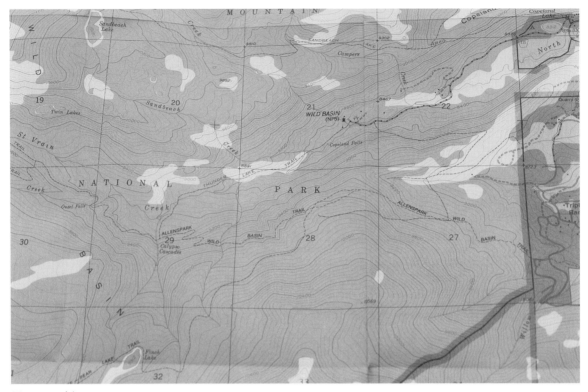

Topographic map.

changes in the trail. Without looking at the map, try to determine which direction you're walking. Then look at the map and see if you are correct. When you take a break, look at the topo map and locate prominent features on the landscape, like a mountain top, a stream, or a wetland. It's a good idea to get used to reading a map and an equally good idea to make a mental note of landmarks you pass during your hike. Practice these techniques on day hikes in familiar places.

Compass Skills

A basic compass weighs only ounces and costs about $7. Obtain a compass and familiarize yourself with its features. Refer to the diagram at right. Don't think you'll ever use it on a backpacking trip? Maybe you'll never need to. But maybe one day you'll take a wrong turn. Maybe a trail marker will be misleading or missing and you'll want to make sure you're on the right track. Maybe your map won't show all the trails in the area and you'll

come to a confusing junction. Maybe you'll come across someone on the trail who needs medical help and you'll need to find the quickest way out of the woods. Maybe a rockslide will destroy part of the trail and you'll have to bushwhack around it to reconnect with the trail. In each of these scenarios, a compass will come in handy.

Community centers, outdoor clubs, parks and recreation departments, or open space departments sometimes offer map and compass courses. Numerous books are available that will show you in great detail what can be done with a map and compass. I'll refer you to one of those sources to develop a more comprehensive understanding of orienteering (see appendix 5). In this book, we'll focus on the basics.

The most fundamental compass exercise is walking a bearing. Let's do that together.

For this exercise, all you need is a compass. Here's the situation: your goal is to hike to a clearing on the ridge in front of you, but there's a dip in the landscape and a dense forest between you and the

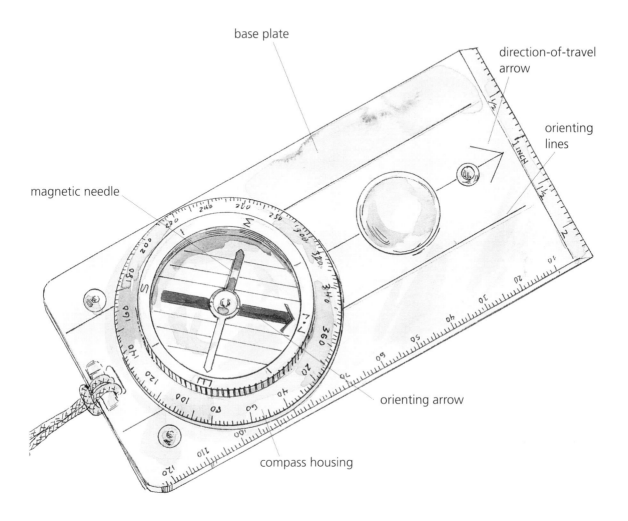

base plate

direction-of-travel arrow

orienting lines

magnetic needle

orienting arrow

compass housing

A basic compass.

clearing. Start by pointing the direction-of-travel arrow at the clearing. Turn the compass housing until the red end of the magnetic needle is aligned with the orienting arrow. Remember "red in the shed" to remind you that it is the red part of the arrow you are interested in. Now read your bearing on the dial. A bearing is a measure of degrees.

Pick an object like a large tree that is in line with your bearing and walk toward it. When you get there, take another sighting along the bearing you've been walking and walk toward it. Even

when you're in the thick of the forest and can no longer see the clearing, if you walk your bearing, you will arrive at the clearing in no time.

Learning how to use a compass will improve your confidence and security in the backcountry, and for many people it can become a hobby. Special courses can show you how to put the map and compass together and how to master more involved orienteering skills. Have fun with it and enjoy the challenge of staying found!

ON THE TRAIL

This section discusses skills and techniques you are likely to use every day on a backpacking trip. They are the skills you will apply as you walk along the trail and the techniques you can use to make the walking more enjoyable.

TRAIL MARKINGS

Most backpackers pick a trail and stick to it. Rarely will you have to leave the trail and forge your own way (unless that is the goal of the trip). Most trails are clearly marked from the trailhead. Signs along the way give distances to points of interest like trail junctions, lakes, mountain tops, or campsites. On the majority of your trips, the trail will be well defined and easy to follow. But there may be times when the trail is not well maintained and signs have been broken or vandalized. During these times, locating the trail may require some attention to trail markings.

Most trails are marked with blazes, cairns, or posts. Blazes are vertical stripes painted on trees just above eye level or on rocks along the trail. Sometimes metal emblems have been nailed to trees in place of blazes. At trail junctions, be sure to continue to follow blazes or emblems of the same shape and color because a specific blaze designates each trail—the Appalachian Trail blaze, for example, is white. In most blazing systems, two blazes indicate a sharp change in direction or a junction of trails; in either case, a double blaze essentially means "be alert!" In one common double blazing system, the blazes are stacked vertically, and the top blaze, which is

A double blaze indicates a sharp turn or trail junction. A turn can be signified by two vertically stacked blazes (left) or by two side-by-side blazes (right).

either to the right or left of the bottom blaze, shows you which direction the trail will turn; another system places the double blaze on the side of the trail *opposite* to the direction of the turn (double blazes on right side of trail indicate a left turn). If you're hiking in unfamiliar territory, take a little time to examine a trail map and become familiar with the local blaze colors and blazing system.

When there are no trees on which to paint blazes (for example, on a treeless ridge, a meadow, or in an alpine or desert environment), cairns or posts are often used. Cairns are piles of rocks that mark the route. From each cairn or post, you should be able to spot the next one. If you don't see it right away, the trail may have changed direction. Spend a moment locating the next cairn or post on the horizon before you leave the one beside you. If there is no distinct trail, avoid setting out on a blind search for posts or cairns. If no marker is in sight, break out the map and compass to make sure you're traveling in the right direction.

Ascending

On one of your forays into the backcountry, you may come across terrain that seems a bit unforgiving. When you tackle the steep stuff, the following tips will make the going a little easier. Your legs have been carrying the load thus far; why not put your arms to work too? Use trekking poles to help propel your body up the mountain—they work tremendously well.

On steep ascents, some hikers like to travel in short bursts and stop often. If that technique works well for you, go for it. Traveling in short bursts causes me to get tired early in the day; I've found that I can travel for longer periods of time and cover more ground if I take the slow and steady approach. You may prefer that approach as well.

As you propel your body up a steep incline, get in the habit of listening to the rhythm of your

cairn

Piles of rocks, called cairns, *mark the trail.*

Descending

On steep descents, your knees can take quite a beating. Trekking poles can take a substantial amount of weight off your knees, provide you with extra stability, and make steep descents more comfortable. When descending, keep your legs slightly bent so your knees don't lock, and rest often. Injuries happen most often when we get tired and careless.

Whether you use poles or not, there are three ways to safely descend a steep slope. The first technique is to walk sideways down the mountain. Keep your knees bent and lean into the slope. If you prefer to walk straight down, approach the descent using one of two methods. You can kick your heels into the slope or you can flex your ankles and make contact with the earth with your entire foot. Keep your weight forward so your feet don't slide out from under you. It may be comforting to know, however, that if you do fall backward, your backpack will provide a softer landing than the ground.

SETTING A PACE

It's often helpful to know how many miles you can cover in a certain amount of time. For instance, let's say there are three hours of daylight left, and you're trying to decide whether you should set up camp at the lake 4 miles down the trail or shoot for the stream 8 miles down the trail. If you know that you hike 2 miles an hour, you will decide to stop at the lake because it will be dark by the time you'd reach the stream.

To find your pace, time how long it takes you to hike 1 mile on both gentle and steep terrain. Compare that figure with your average pace at the end of the day. Notice the difference. For example, in the morning I determine that it takes me one

Trekking poles help propel your body up mountains, and they give your knees a break on steep descents.

breath. Breathing sounds like such a simple thing to do, but different breathing styles can significantly affect your performance. Time every step or every second or third step with an exhale. Exhale and inhale fully. Try breathing through your nose; this will help slow down your breath. If you can coordinate your breath with your steps, you may be able to enter a trancelike state in which you are aware that your body is working but you are comfortable with it.

Three ways to descend a slope. Left: Turn sideways and step with your knees bent. Middle: Dig your heels into the earth. Right: Flex your ankles and walk down slowly.

hour to walk 3 miles. I hike for five hours that day and cover a total distance of 10 miles (that's a pace of 2 miles per hour—10 ÷ 5 = 2). If my pace was really 3 miles an hour, I should have covered 15 miles. It's important to consider how much time you spend taking breaks. I took a few long breaks throughout the day, which is why my short-term pace was 3 miles per hour and my cumulative pace was 2 miles per hour.

By examining how long it takes you to travel a specified distance in different scenarios (when you're tired, at the end of the day, on technical terrain, when your pack weighs only a fifth of your body weight), you will get a rough idea of your pace under different conditions. Your pace will change with the terrain, the goals of your trip, and your fitness, but a rough estimate ought

to be fairly easy to come by. If all this calculation does not seem to be compatible with the idea of hiking, don't do it—it can simply be a tool for those who like to keep track of time and distance.

In a Group

Whatever your hiking style, keep track of others you are hiking with. Don't expect everyone in your group to travel at the same pace. Some hikers start out at top speed while others gradually work into a rhythm. Some people prefer to rest often, while others like to walk for hours without stopping. Find a pace that feels good to you, but don't leave a slower hiker in the dust and abandon him or her for most of the day. Don't let others run away without you, either. If the person or people with whom you are traveling have very different paces, choose an obvious place (like a lake or a trail junction) or a time to stop and regroup.

When traveling with a group, get in the habit of stopping at *all* trail junctions and potentially confusing spots along the trail. No matter how obvious it looks to you, it is easy to stray off the main path if you've let your mind wander for too long. All members of the group should have food, water, and shelter in case they get separated from the group. If there is a large disparity in the abilities within the group, give the speediest hikers the most weight and let those who move more slowly carry lighter packs. Everyone in the group ought to have a say in the planning process and ought to be familiar with the map and the group's itinerary. Don't rely on others to plan the route and figure that you'll just follow along; always know where you're going and what the terrain will be like.

In the event that you become separated from your hiking party, the first thing you should do is stop. Take as long as you need to retrace the trail in your mind and note if there was a fork or a junction where you might have gone astray. If you have a map, try to figure out where you are. If you think you know how to get back on track, go for it, but keep a written record of your efforts. Note how far and in what direction you are traveling. Record landmarks such as bridges, rivers, meadows, and large rocks. In case your plan fails, you will be able to return to your original location. The worst thing you can do is wander aimlessly and try different approaches—you will likely get even more disoriented, and it will make it nearly impossible for anyone to locate you.

When in doubt, stay put. Periodically shout or blow a whistle to signal to others who may be looking for you. Drink plenty of water, find adequate shelter for the night, and light a smoky fire to indicate your position to searchers.

FORDING RIVERS

You are likely to encounter a river on many of your backcountry outings. Of course, you'll know this ahead of time because you've studied the topographic map of the area. When a trail crosses a river, there is often a narrow footbridge or a log to help you get across. Many times the bridge will be wide and stable, and you'll feel comfortable

Fording a river can be an exhilarating part of a backpacking trip.

crossing it. If the bridge looks unstable or if it is very narrow, use your best judgment. If balancing on a log seems dangerous (especially if it is narrow, wet, or more than a couple of feet above the ground), either slide or crawl across, or ford the river. In places where a bridge or log crossing seems dangerous or doesn't exist, you'll have to cross the river on your own.

Fording rivers can be fun, but you want to do it the safest way possible. A word of caution: if the river seems especially swift or deep, or if you get an uneasy feeling about the ford, don't attempt to cross it. Keep in mind that many mountain streams are lower in the morning and that the current often moves more slowly in the widest part of the river. To test the depth of the water, toss grapefruit-sized rocks in the river. A hollow "kerplunk" means the water is deep. If you hear the rock hit the bottom, the water is probably less than knee-deep. If the water is below your knee and seems crossable, then attempt the ford. I always ford rivers wearing sandals or old sneakers. It's impractical to get your hiking boots wet, and it's dangerous to walk across in your bare feet because the river bottom may be slippery or contain sharp rocks.

Begin the ford by unclasping your hipbelt. On the off-chance that you slip, you may want to quickly get out of your backpack. If the hipbelt is unclasped, you will be able to slide out of the backpack more easily. If you're not carrying trekking poles, find a stick. Having some sort of staff will help you balance as you work your way across. Face slightly upstream and focus on an object on the opposite bank. You may become dizzy if you stare at the current. Feel the river bottom with your feet, and don't commit to a step unless it feels secure. Take your time and use your hiking stick for support.

Many streams are bridged by a single log.

Cross deep, swift rivers in a group. The following technique works well with two to five people. Have everyone in your group line up one behind the other, facing upstream with the tallest person in the front; he or she should have a hiking stick for support. The hikers behind the first one should be close enough together as the group steps into the river that each can lean forward into the backpack of the person in front of them. As the current pushes each person backward, the next person leans forward into the backpack, leaning hard enough to counter the force of the current but not so much as to push the person forward. It's important for your line to move as a unit, so designate one person to yell "Step . . . and step . . . and step . . . ," as everyone shuffles sideways across the river in unison. Using this technique I've felt relatively secure crossing rivers well above my waist.

Cross deep rivers in a group. Hold on to the person in front of you and shuffle across sideways in unison.

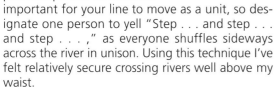

TRAIL ETIQUETTE

You may have heard about Leave No Trace guidelines, minimum-impact camping, and low-impact hiking. These terms refer to a way of interacting with the environment and other hikers in a responsible way. Outdoor recreationists are putting tremendous strain on the backcountry because so many of us want to recreate in the same places. I know of a small lake where dozens of people in a single weekend vie for fishing and camping opportunities. Every weekend, a string of climbers ascends a popular peak near my home, and I can see a city of tents sprawled across the wildflower meadow at its base.

When you're surrounded by a landscape that is seemingly endless, it's easy to think that the actions of one person could not possibly make a difference. But they can, and they do. The shore of the small lake has become trampled. Rare plants along the trail up the popular mountain had to be fenced off, and the trail is being rerouted. After patches of green wore away to dirt in the wildflower meadow, the meadow was closed to camping.

In heavily traveled areas, fire pits serve as garbage dumps; shelters and trail markers have been vandalized; and authorities are forced to close areas to recreation. Acting responsibly can be a win-win situation for everyone. Impacts to the resource can be minimal and everyone's experiences can be enjoyable if we follow a few trail etiquette guidelines. Treat the resource with respect, and there is less likelihood that your access will be restricted. Interact responsibly with the environment and your favorite places will remain wild and beautiful.

Minimum-Impact Guidelines

Stay on the Trail

Don't cut straight up the side of a mountain if the trail meanders back and forth. Those meanders, or switchbacks, were constructed to prevent the trail from eroding. Also stay on the trail to avoid trampling vegetation and soils that, especially in alpine and desert ecosystems, can take decades to form. Wear appropriate footwear so you can walk through muddy sections of trail. When hikers create alternate paths around muddy sections, they widen the trail and trample the vegetation. Volunteers spend a lot of time restoring widened trails to narrow footpaths.

Step off the Trail for Rest Breaks

When you take a rest break, step off the trail so other hikers don't have to crawl over you and your gear.

Choose a durable surface on which to rest, like a rock slab or a patch of duff under a pine tree. After you've had a snack, pack out every scrap. I like to use a resealable plastic bag as a garbage bag. I store it in an external pouch on my backpack so it is easy to access and stays away from my clothes and food.

Washing Face and Hands

Be careful not to wash your hands or face in a lake or stream if you have applied bug repellent or sunscreen.

Such products are toxic to the aquatic critters whose home you are using as a bath. Go ahead, take a dip in the lake (you deserve it!), but before you take the plunge, take a few seconds to carry a jug of water away from the lake and rinse off.

Marking Your Route

Don't mark your route with string or piles of rocks.

Use a map and compass to check your direction of travel, and communicate with your partners exactly where you are going.

Leave Wildlife Alone

Please don't attempt to feed wildlife, and don't let your children torment or torture animals (including insects!).

Feeding wildlife ultimately harms them (because animals that become dependent on humans

In addition to preventing erosion, switchbacks make it easier to climb up and down.

Cutting switchbacks not only wastes energy but can lead to severe erosion and trail closures.

and plants on many public lands without a permit.

Leave the Phone at Home

I strongly recommend that you leave all signs of technology—cellular phones, laptop computers, portable music players, and other similar items—at home

Leaving society behind and experiencing an alternative way of living are what make backpacking so special. Keep in mind that what you might perceive as a link to safety or to your work may be an intrusion to others. For some backpackers, hearing a phone ring or listening to music degrades their wilderness experience because it diminishes a sense of detachment from civilization and feelings (either real or perceived) of self-sufficiency. Rescuers have found that hikers who carry cellular phones are likely to take risks they normally wouldn't take. Cell phone users maintain a false sense of security because the phone does not guarantee a connection to civilization. Rescuers are increasingly less willing to initiate rescues for people who are not in life-threatening situations or who have acted irresponsibly or carelessly. If you insist on bringing your cell phone, please don't use it in front of other hikers, especially in places where hikers are likely to congregate (on mountain tops, in shelters, or at popular campsites).

Horses and Cyclists

The general rule on multiple-use trails is that hikers yield to horses. When a horse approaches, step off the trail (on the downslope, if possible) and let the horse pass by. Bikers are supposed to yield to hikers, although I usually step out of the way if a cyclist is working really hard on a steep climb. Acting courteously will enhance everyone's experience.

are often considered pests and will be shot by local wildlife officials), and it can be dangerous to you, too. Wild animals can become dependent on humans and act aggressively toward people if they realize humans supply food. Also keep in mind that it's illegal to collect feathers, antlers, rocks, bones,

AT CAMP

These are the skills and techniques you'll use when you're ready to stop for the day, when you decide it's time to claim a spot to call "home" for the night. Having a handle on the following techniques will help you make the most of your time at camp.

CHOOSING A CAMPSITE

As you begin each day of your backpacking trip, you will probably have a destination in mind, such as an established camping area or a landmark like a lake or a clearing that is easy to find and close to water. When I reach my destination, I like to take my backpack off, grab a snack, and leisurely begin the search for the perfect campsite.

A number of factors make a campsite desirable. Ideally you would like to find a place that is level—a spot where the ground is smooth and soft; where water is close by; where a gentle breeze creates the ideal temperature inside the tent; where water quickly percolates through the soil and flows away from your tent; and where you can enjoy scenic views but not be exposed to the elements.

It may take some time to find the right place, so don't get discouraged if you don't decide where to settle within thirty seconds of arriving at the lake. During your travels you will find good campsites. In fact, you will probably find sites with scenery that will knock your socks off, and you'll

Ideal campsites are hard to come by. Cherish the moment when you find one!

Best and Worst Campsites

I've seen a lot of campsites in my backpacking career; some have been better than others. I'd like to share with you my top two best and worst campsites. Topping the list for the worst campsite ever is a spot in New Jersey. I had wandered into an area that I thought was more remote than it actually was. Nearby roads made the area accessible to urban hikers, and the camping area was at full capacity by three in the afternoon. Troops of Scouts erected a city of tents across the little meadow, the outhouse had overflowed, and one group of rowdy campers was drinking beer and singing into the wee hours of the morning. The train tracks weren't visible from my tent site, so in the middle of the night when I heard the deafening sound of wheels grating on metal tracks and felt the ground shake, I was certain the train was headed directly for my tent.

The second worst site is a spot essentially in the middle of a bog. When I camped there, I had to stay in my tent the entire time or endure the onslaught of mosquitoes. The ground was wet and lumpy, and the air was hot and humid. With a cloud of mosquitoes in hot pursuit, I ran to the water source to find a puddle of brown, stagnant water. The next morning, I left as quickly as I could.

The best spot I ever camped on is a flat, grassy meadow at about 11,000 feet. It was a cool, still night, and the Milky Way stretched across the black sky. A herd of elk nestled in the tall grasses just 500 feet below my perch. Warm sunshine nudged me out of bed, and I lingered among the wildflowers for most of the morning, sipping hot tea as the songbirds made their rounds.

My other special spot is on the Oregon coast. While I was there, the sea breeze mixed salty ocean fragrance with the smell of my curry dinner. I ate as a smear of pink and orange spread across the sky. There's nothing like sleeping on sand and being lulled to sleep by lapping waves.

have mornings where you wake up thinking, "That was the best night's sleep I've had in a long time." But you will rarely find a *perfect* site. Yes, keep striving to find that magical spot, the one where topography, temperature, humidity, and wind speed create perfect camping conditions. Keep in mind that there are maybe ten such places on the planet. Most of the time, one or two minor adjustments will have to be made or one or two not-so-perfect things will have to be dealt with.

There may be a small lump under the tent. No problem; that's why you're carrying a sleeping mattress. You may choose to sacrifice the 360-degree view to avoid sleeping on a ridge where hurricane-force gales will rattle the tent. You may have to walk a quarter mile to the water source, but that's why you're carrying a water bag—so you have to make only one trip.

The most important consideration when choosing a campsite is "level and smooth" or, if rain is possible, "somewhere that will stay dry." Look for a place that can withstand a beating, like grasses or a clearing of pine needles. As a general rule, camp at least 200 feet from the water source and 200 feet from the trail. This will give you some privacy, and basically, it's the polite thing to do. Never try to alter the site to accommodate you or your tent; never dig trenches around the tent to funnel rain, and don't cut branches to make more room. Work with what you have.

PITCHING THE TENT

Remember these words of wisdom: learn how to pitch your tent at home. Also, check your tent's stuff sack before you leave to make sure that the tent, rainfly, ground cloth, poles, and stakes are all in the bag. You don't want to be fumbling in the dark with the tent poles and rainfly, wondering how to erect your shelter; or worse, you don't want to get to camp and realize that half the tent is still in the closet at home.

Read carefully the instructions on how to pitch your tent. They will vary depending on the tent, although most models follow a similar procedure. Lay the tent on the ground. Straighten the collapsible tent poles and slip them through

Pitching the tent is an important skill to learn. Lay the tent on the ground and assemble the poles. Connect the poles to the tent and it will pop into shape.

the sleeves of the tent or, if your tent sports clips instead of sleeves, clip in the poles. Insert the ends of the poles into the grommets at the base of the tent, and the tent will pop into shape. Many tents are freestanding; that is, they will hold their form once the poles are in place. Other tents must be staked or tied or both. For increased stability, and to avoid having your tent blow away, stake a tent even if it's freestanding. Slip a stake through a strap or grommet at the base of the tent, pull the tent material taut, and gently tap the stake into the ground using a rock.

If it is particularly cool, if rain is possible, or if you simply like the idea of sleeping beneath a rainfly, go ahead and secure the fly. This usually involves fastening the fly to the base of the tent where the poles attach. Pull the fly taut and stake the fly to prevent the material from sagging into the tent. The tighter the fly, the better it will be at deflecting rain. If the fly sags into the tent material, water may seep through, and you'll have a leak in the middle of the night.

CAMPING IN TENT

It is always better to stop early if the weather looks threatening or hide out until the storm passes, but there may be a time or two when setting up camp in the rain is unavoidable. When this happens, there are a number of things you can do to keep you and your gear as dry as possible while setting up camp.

Your first priority should be to keep your gear dry. If you carry a tarp in addition to a tent, string the tarp first, pile your gear under it, and if there's room, pitch the tent beneath the tarp. Tarps are excellent additions to your standard shelter. Use one as an extended vestibule once the tent is erected. They serve as excellent storage areas, and they make cooking in the rain a simple task.

If you don't bring a tarp, you can still stay relatively dry. Here's what I do. Remove the tent from the pack and immediately cover the backpack with its pack fly and stash it under a tree. Spread the tent on top of the ground cloth and immediately cover it with the rainfly. It is a little awkward to thread the poles under the rainfly, but you'll get the hang of it. Erect the tent, secure the fly, and make sure the ground cloth is completely under the tent floor. I then throw most of my gear inside the shel-ter, place the backpack and boots on top of the backpack fly and stick them in the vestibule, and then I dive in.

CAMPFIRES

In many places, campfires have become relics of the past. Because of fire hazards and overuse, campfires are illegal in many backcountry locations, and officials prefer that you use backcountry stoves for all your cooking needs. Although you will always carry a stove, every now and then you will be in a place that is not too windy or not too dry and that has abundant downed wood, and you will want to build a campfire. Inquire at the ranger station or with local officials about fire regulations and current conditions in the area through which you will be traveling. If it is legal to build a campfire and if the conditions are safe for one, go for it, but follow these guidelines to keep the fire under control and to minimally affect your surroundings.

If a fire ring exists, use it. If you construct a fire ring by placing rocks in a circle, dismantle the ring and scatter the rocks when you're finished using it. Fire rings can be an eyesore, and they tend to encourage people to have fires. Also, negligent hikers tend to think of fire circles as trash pits, which they are not.

When you build a fire, keep it small. Use kindling to start it, and burn pieces of wood that have less than a 2-inch diameter. Never cut tree limbs; use wood you find on the ground.

Never leave a fire unattended. Burn the wood to ash, and before you go to bed, make sure the fire is completely out by dousing the area with water.

Use great care when building a fire in the backcountry. It is easier than you might think for a small campfire to turn into a disaster.

WASHING DISHES

You've prepared your meal and devoured it with the appetite of a true backpacker. Now it's time to clean up. Here are a few suggestions about cleaning cookware. The first point (which, in my experience, is moot on most backpacking trips) is to eat all the food you prepare. It is quite difficult to store leftovers, so make a point to accurately estimate the amount of food to prepare, and clean your plate. If by some chance you cannot finish the portion, the proper thing to do is to store leftovers in an extra bag or water jug for the night and finish it the next day. If you would rather not experience the marginal-to-begin-with beef stew the second time around, pack it out in a resealable plastic bag. Unless you've created some horrendous concoction, finishing food shouldn't be a problem.

Now you're left with a dirty pot or two. Do not, I repeat, do not take your pot to the stream, lather up, and turn the stream into your kitchen sink. Instead, retrieve water from the stream and bring it to your cooking site. Most cookware can be cleaned without soap, especially on short trips, but if you insist on bringing soap, use soap identified as "biodegradable" (purchase from an outdoors or sporting goods store). Even biodegradable soap does not decompose in water, which is why you should never wash dishes in a water source, especially one from which you are also getting your drinking water!

Bring the water to your cooking area, scrub the pot, and discard the wastewater at least 150 feet from the water source. I don't carry soap or a sponge. It saves weight to leave those items at home. I scrub my pots with pine cones or gravel. Feathery spruce or Douglas fir cones work best! If the natural method is not your first choice, bring a tiny bottle of biodegradable soap and either a small sponge or a bandanna. Every couple of days, sterilize your cookware and utensils with boiling water.

STORING FOOD SAFE

Animals can be attracted to a number of smells that we bring into the woods. In addition to food, animals can be attracted to scented items like suntan lotion and toothpaste. Animals such as deer, skunks, and porcupines will chew on anything salty, like your hiking shirt and hiking boots. So, when you store your food for the night, consider storing more than your food.

I usually store two stuff sacks at night: one bag contains my food and my trash bag, and the other contains toiletries. In areas that may have bears, I store my stove and cookware with the toiletries. I keep my salty clothes in the tent and store my boots in the vestibule.

In some places, it may be OK to store food in your tent (if you're in an area where wildlife is not an issue—bears are not found in the Great Plains, for example). A ranger can advise you whether sleeping with your food is a good idea or not. In many backcountry locations, especially in places with bears, it is a very bad idea to sleep with your food. In bear country, keeping food (or anything scented) in a tent can be dangerous.

At campsites in some areas, bear boxes, bear canisters, or bear poles are provided. A bear box is a metal locker that provides safe storage for your food and toiletries, and it is quite convenient. At popular destinations, bear boxes fill quickly, so it's a good idea to have a backup plan.

A bear canister is a bear-proof cylinder that you carry in your backpack. You fill the canister with food and lock it. At night, stash the canister away from your tent. If a bear should discover the canister, it won't be able to open it. Canisters are often sold or rented at ranger stations or outfitting stores adjacent to hiking destinations in bear country. Although a canister will add weight to your pack, the security is well worth it.

In many areas, the managing agency provides poles and a pulley system from which to hang your food. Like the bear boxes, they are very convenient and they don't require that you carry any additional gear.

If none of these is provided, the best way to store food is to hang your food and toiletry bags with parachute cord. Parachute cord is very lightweight and durable. Here's what you do. Find a limb that is about 20 feet off the ground and that looks like it will be sturdy enough to support the weight of your food and toiletries but might not support the weight of a small bear. Attach your bag to one end of the cord and toss it over the limb. Tie a second bag (of relatively equal weight) as high as you can on the other end of the cord. Use a stick to push the bag up. The bags should be at least 10 feet from the tree trunk, and they should be dangling about 5 feet from the branch. In the morning, use the stick to retrieve the bag. It's easier if you tie a loop on the cord near the bag so you can easily snag it with the stick.

Secure a food bag to the end of the rope and throw it over the branch. Tie a second bag as high as you can on the rope. Push the lower bag up with a stick until the bags are hanging at the same height.

Smaller critters like mice may want to rummage through your gear at night, and I usually let them. I leave the pouches on my backpack open and un-zipped so they won't have to chew holes through the material to get inside (believe me, they'll get in-side whether you unzip the pockets or not!).

CAMPING ETIQUETTE

Practicing minimum-impact camping skills is an ex-cellent way to enhance your experience and the experiences of those around you. A few basic guidelines should be followed in every back-packer's camp.

Start by choosing a campsite that is at least 200 feet from the trail, the water source, and other campers (unless designated sites are closer to-gether). Do this to maintain a sense of solitude and isolation for you and the people around you. If you have a brightly colored tent, conceal it as best you can by tucking it behind a group of trees or shrubs.

At camp, refrain from using a cell phone or ra-dio in earshot of other campers. Again, it is best if you leave these items at home.

Tread lightly along stream corridors, called ripar-ian zones.

As always, whatever comes out of your pack at camp goes with you when you leave the site. Don't forget the socks you left drying on the rock, or the empty plastic bag, or the extra food.

The green areas around wetlands, springs, ponds, lakes, and streams are called *riparian zones*. These zones play a critical role in every ecosystem: they provide habitat for fish and wildlife, they control floods, they filter sediment and enhance water quality, and they are extremely rich and productive. They are also very fragile—wet streambanks get trampled and erode easily. Understand the importance of these areas and tread lightly when you go there. Making one or two trips to the water source will save you energy and minimize your impact on the environment.

If you bring pets, keep them under control at all times and don't let them play in the water source or antagonize other campers. (Information about backpacking with dogs is in chapter 10, Taking the Dog.)

HYGIENE

Throughout this book, I've urged you to carry only the basics. In case there is still some doubt, I'll make it perfectly clear: Leave the razors and shaving cream, perfume and cologne, shampoo and conditioner, bath towel and wash cloth, deodorant, makeup, and jewelry at home. This is my rule of thumb: If an item is not in some way contributing to my survival (that is, it doesn't help me eat, be sheltered, or stay warm and hydrated), or if I don't use it every day, it stays out of my pack. As an extra incentive to leave the beauty products at home, know that mosquitoes are attracted to fresh-smelling humans!

Keeping it simple doesn't mean that you have to neglect basic hygiene. You can expect to get dirty on a backpacking trip, but you don't have to feel filthy all the time. Accept the fact that a backcountry wipe-down will not leave you feeling as though you stepped out of a steaming shower, but know that there are a few basic things you can do to maintain good hygiene in the outdoors. For starters, bring a clean shirt and clean socks to change into when you arrive at camp. Changing out of dirty, sweaty clothes is a tremendous pleasure, and I promise you'll instantly feel cleaner. Sleeping in a fresh shirt will also keep your sleeping bag looking and smelling fresh.

Washing Clothes

Because you are not going to bring a lot of clothes on your trip (remember, you're keeping it simple, right?), you may have to wash some items from time to time, especially on longer trips. There are a couple of things you should know about doing laundry. First, don't wash your clothes if it is raining or if you need to wear them the next morning and it's 30 degrees out—they're not going to dry. Don't subject yourself to the agony of lugging wet clothes through the mountains. It is easier to endure a little stink than it is to endure the weight of 10 pounds of wet laundry.

If it's sunny and warm, and you'd like to wash your second pair of socks or your hiking shirt, go for it. But don't do it directly in the stream or lake. Even biodegradable soap won't degrade in water, and you certainly don't want to flush into the pristine lake the toxic bug spray that's on your shirt.

Here's how you do it. Bring water to the clothing: fill your bladder bag, your water jugs, your cooking pots, whatever you prefer. Lather up and scrub your clothes clean, but do it away from the water source and scatter the wastewater at least 200 feet from the source.

Bathing

Most backpackers save the full-fledged shower for the end of the trip, when they're in the comfort of their own home. Bathing in the backcountry can be a challenge because the water is usually cold. In fact, it can be downright frigid! To make bathing more comfortable, some hikers hang a bladder bag in the sun until the water warms up, then they use the spout as a shower head and take a quick one.

For most of us, a quick rinse will have to suffice. When you wash your hands and face, use treated water. Or try the antiseptic towelettes that you use to clean up after eating a rack of ribs at a barbecue. If you opt for the full body scrub-down, bring the water to you; don't use soap or wash off sunscreen directly in the stream. Give yourself a quick rinse far from the source so wastewater doesn't run off into the lake during the next rainstorm. The same goes if you plan to take a swim. Rinse the toxic stuff off your body at least 200 feet from the lake before you start doing laps.

Teeth

Biodegradable soap is a multipurpose soap, recommended for washing your body, your clothes, your cookware, and your teeth. As toothpaste, however, it's a heck of a good dish soap! Catch my drift? Bring your own toothpaste.

When you brush, remember to use only water that has been treated. To cut weight, bring a tiny tube of toothpaste or repackage it in a small container.

In every instance, I've advised you to discard wastewater at least 200 feet from the water source. It is an equally good idea to discard wastewater from washing your body, your clothes, pots and pans, and your teeth a good distance (say 200 feet) from your sleeping areas. Animals such as bears are attracted to scents of food or toothpaste that may linger in wastewater. If animals are going to find your food scraps and toothpaste spit,

better that they find them a good distance from your tent!

Hair

If you have short hair, feel free to neglect it the entire trip. There is something marvelous about surrendering your vanity! Feel free to neglect your long hair, too, although sometimes it's easier to tie it up to keep it out of your face. Braids work well in the backcountry, and a small comb will take care of the knots. Use a bandanna to tame unruly hair and to keep sweat from dripping in your eyes.

I've never washed my hair on a backpacking trip; I don't see much point to it. But if you would like to try, I recommend No-Rinse Shampoo, manufactured by N/R Laboratories. That way, you don't have to worry about polluting a water source.

Hygiene Kit

Where should you keep all these products? In a personal hygiene kit, of course. I use a resealable plastic bag for my toothbrush and tiny tube of

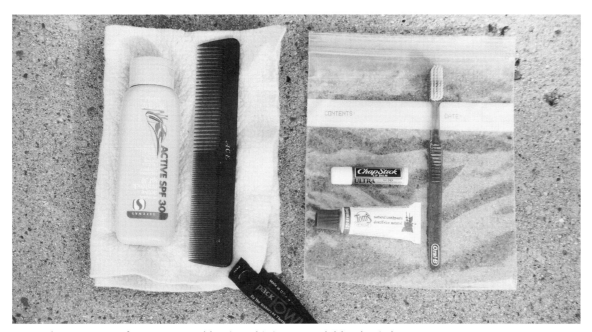

Store the contents of your personal hygiene kit in a resealable plastic bag.

toothpaste, comb and a hair tie, lip balm, sunscreen, and a bandanna.

Natural Waste

We've reached the point in the course where we need to address some sensitive issues. There's no need to get embarrassed about bodily functions; we all go to the bathroom, and when you go backpacking, you'll have to go in the woods. Better be prepared so you know what you're doing.

There are a few simple rules of etiquette to follow when you're peeing in the woods. The first is that you should literally pee in the woods. Don't relieve yourself on the trail. Other hikers will appreciate your moving entirely out of view from the trail.

Second, do not go to the bathroom near cooking areas or near water sources; you should be at least 150 feet from them to avoid contaminating them.

Finally, choose a nonvegetative surface on which to pee. Dirt and rock are good choices because animals are sometimes attracted to urine and will dig up plants that have been sprayed.

There is actually an entire book written about our next item of business. It's called *How to Shit in the Woods* by Kathleen Meyer (I bet you didn't think it could be so complicated!). The book is quite entertaining and delivers some very useful information about affecting the environment minimally when you relieve yourself in the backcountry. If you want details, find that publication. For now, I'll cover the basics.

Let's run through the basic procedure. You gotta go. You take off your backpack and remove two resealable plastic bags and a small trowel (trowels are metal or plastic and are used to dig small holes). One bag contains a partial roll of toilet paper, and the other bag is empty.

Now start walking. The spot you choose is critical. The idea is to get at least 200 feet from everything: from other hikers, campsites, the trail, and especially water. Choose an area where rain is not likely to wash your waste down a slope and into a creek. As you approach a good-looking spot, grab a stick off the ground (this will come in handy in a few minutes). In most environs you will want to dig a 4- to 8-inch hole in which you will bury the fecal matter. Pooping in a hole facilitates decompo-

sition because it brings the fecal matter into contact with the bacteria in the soil. Burying it also prevents other hikers from encountering something that is not aesthetically appealing.

Digging a hole works best in rich organic soils and in damp climes. If you are backpacking in a desert or in a dry place with very shallow rocky soils, the smearing technique is preferred. The smearing technique works like this: find a nice flat rock, do your business on it, then take a rock or stick and smear the waste over the rock. In such areas, waste will decompose more quickly if it's exposed to the sun than it will if it is buried. Your waste will dry out and flake off the rock. The smear method is acceptable only when you are not in a populated area. If there is a chance that another camper will encounter your smeared rock, it may be best to bury it.

So, let's say the soils are deep and rich and you've dug a 6-inch hole with a trowel, a stick, or your heel. After you've relieved yourself, take out the resealable plastic bags. One bag contains toilet paper, and the empty bag will soon contain used toilet paper. Never bury the toilet paper; it is best to pack it out and flush it down the toilet once you get home. Also refrain from burning the toilet paper, which can be a fire hazard (unless you burn it in a controlled campfire, and your hiking partners don't mind).

You may want to consider not bringing toilet paper at all. There are many other natural substitutes, and they don't have to be packed out! Try using leaves, grasses, moss, or pine cones. At first, these methods may sound a bit crude, but don't knock 'em 'til you've tried 'em!

Now take out the stick you picked up earlier. It's important to mix the fecal matter with the soils so the bacteria can get to work, so give the contents in your hole a good stir, toss the stick, and cover the hole. When you leave the spot, it should look as though no one had been there.

FOR WOMEN ONLY

I've identified two areas in which a woman's trip differs from a man's. The first is the simple act of peeing. Often it is no problem to take off your backpack, find an appropriate spot, and take care of business. But sometimes it's very inconvenient to have to remove your backpack to pee. On trips in cooler weather, or if you're hiking across a windy ridge, it can be dangerous to remove your pack and let the cold breeze freeze your wet shirt to your back. It is certainly uncomfortable! And we are all about comfort when we go backpacking. The key then, is to pee without removing your backpack.

Once you've found a spot, unclasp your hipbelt and wriggle your shorts off your hips. If your legs are fresh and strong, you may be able to perform an unassisted squat. If balancing in a squat with a backpack is too much, squat behind a small tree and hold on to the trunk for support.

Regardless of how you choose to squat, you obviously want to keep your feet dry, which can be a challenge because, let's face it, you can spread your feet only so far. The trick is to put your feet on two rocks and pee in the middle of them. If rocks aren't available, try standing on anything that is slightly raised. Pee into a depression and the urine won't run into your boots. Pee on something soft, and it won't splatter. You'll get the hang of it.

The second way our trips differ from men's trips is that from time to time our menstrual cycle will coincide with our trips into the backcountry. As much as we would like to plan trips around our menstrual cycles, it is often not possible. However, having your period on a backpacking trip doesn't have to be a big ordeal, and it certainly won't ruin your trip.

The most important advice I can give you is to be prepared for it on every trip, even if you are certain you won't get it that week. I carry a few tampons in my personal hygiene kit on every trip, just in case.

If you expect to get your period during the trip, bring two extra resealable plastic bags. In the first bag, store tampons or pads or whatever you use to catch the flow. Use the second bag as a garbage bag for used sanitary products. Don't dispose of them in outhouses; they have to be removed by hand when the outhouses are cleaned. Never bury used tampons or pads or discard them in the backcountry; animals will dig them up. Many women prefer to keep the trash bag inside a cloth bag so they don't have to look at the used products. I store the menstrual garbage bag next to the regular garbage bag in an external pocket on my backpack.

There is no documentation that animals such as bears will act aggressively toward menstruating women, but it is best to not attract them with used products. When you set up camp, hang the menstrual trash bag with the regular trash bag; never sleep with it in the tent. To feel fresh and clean, carry a packet of moist, disposable towelettes, antiseptic towelettes, or a soft sponge. I keep them in the bag with the supply of tampons and pads.

FOR MEN ONLY

Although both men and women can experience some form of groin chafing on a backpacking trip, men seem to experience it more often than women. Especially on longer trips, the sweat and the constant rubbing between your legs can produce chafing. This unpleasant condition can be avoided by keeping the area as clean and dry as possible. My male friends tell me that wearing baggy shorts with no underwear is a good way to keep the area well ventilated. You may also want to bring moist antiseptic towelettes or a soft sponge to keep the area clean.

If you experience chafing on a trip, lubricate the affected area with an antibiotic ointment with pain relief (Neosporin, for example) to prevent further chafing and to minimize the discomfort.

SAFE TRAVEL

This chapter presents information on traveling safely through the backcountry. I've identified four categories that could potentially cause you harm: the elements, animals, plants, and other people. In each case, if you're aware of the signs and symptoms of an illness or injury, if you can recognize a potentially dangerous situation and do your best to avoid it, and if you can treat basic injuries and illnesses, your backcountry travels are likely to be safe. Knowing how to respond if you or someone around you gets injured or ill will make you feel more confident in the backcountry.

In the introduction, I talk about being a self-sufficient backpacker. In addition to providing your own food and shelter, being self-sufficient means being able to care for yourself should anything go wrong. Although it's important to spend some time addressing potential threats to your well-being, keep in mind that the odds of your getting injured by another person in the backcountry, being bitten by a poisonous snake, or breaking your leg are exceptionally slim. I address these situations because it's better to be prepared and equipped to handle an emergency should one arise, but remember, you are far safer in the backcountry than you are in an urban area.

THE ELEMENTS

Terrain

Most backpacking injuries result from slipping on technical terrain or scraping your knee against a rock or tree. These injuries can be easily treated if you have some basic knowledge of first aid. Contact your local fire department or Red Cross to find out how you can get certified in first aid and cardiopulmonary resuscitation (CPR). In a half-day first-aid course, you can learn how to prevent injuries, control bleeding, treat muscle, bone, or joint injuries, and treat burns.

If you would like to learn more about treating injuries in the backcountry, I encourage you to take a wilderness first-aid or a wilderness first-responder course. These courses provide an in-depth look at treating injuries in the backcountry when calling 911 is not an option. Many reputable outfits offer advanced medical training (see appendix 5 for contact information).

Your best defense against injury is prevention. To prevent getting blisters, break in your new boots before your trip, and wear synthetic socks and liners. To prevent injuries like twisted ankles or scraped knees, rest often and stop for the day before you become exhausted. Most injuries occur when your body becomes fatigued. As you begin to lose your focus, you start losing your balance and tripping over rocks. To reduce the chance of injury, rest often, stretch, and stay well fed and hydrated.

Unfortunately, even if you take preventive measures, you can still get injured, which is why you ought to journey into the backcountry with some basic first-aid skills and the supplies necessary to treat common injuries.

If you cut or scrape yourself, and if it is not a gushing wound, your first priority should be to clean the wound. Fill the 10-cubic-centimeter syringe from your first-aid kit with treated water and flush the cut until all visible dirt or debris is out of it. Stop the bleeding by covering the wound with a sterile pad and applying pressure.

Your first priority should be to stop extensive bleeding. Put a sterile gauze pad on the wound and apply pressure. If blood soaks through the pad, place another pad on top of the first pad and continue applying pressure. Elevate the injured area above the heart. Eventually wrap the cut with a roller bandage made of gauze or elastic.

If you or your hiking partner experiences an injury to a bone, muscle, or joint, soak the injured part in cold water (such as in a stream) and elevate the injured area. Determine whether the person can continue walking (for example, for a mildly twisted ankle, the person may be able to walk if the ankle is wrapped with an elastic bandage). If the person cannot continue the trip or travel out of the woods, you will need to bring medical help. If you are traveling in a group, have one person stay with the injured person and send two people for help. The person or people going for help should write down information before they leave the site. Record the exact location of the victim, his or her symptoms, age, health concerns, current medication, how and when the injury happened, and what treatment has been performed. If you need to move the injured person, splint the injured area before doing so. This may involve placing a stick or a piece of clothing beside the injured area and wrapping it with an elastic bandage or with a triangular bandage.

Blisters often seem trivial, but they can cause as much pain as a twisted ankle. Fortunately, they are easier to treat. The trick to warding off blisters is to treat them the moment you feel them coming on. We call those early blisters "hot spots." If you feel a hot spot, stop immediately and put a piece of moleskin or other blister protectant over the area. I've found that Band-Aids don't stick well to sweaty feet, and sometimes moleskin falls off as well. If you have problems with bandages staying on your feet, especially on your heels where there is constant friction, try applying iodine solution to the skin before putting on a bandage. Once it dries, iodine should help the bandage stay put. You can also try covering blisters or hot spots with molefoam and narrow strips of duct tape. Duct tape may be difficult to remove, but I prefer duct tape to blisters.

During your hike, try to keep your feet as dry as possible. Dry your feet and socks during rest breaks, and apply powder to your feet to help keep them dry. If you do get a blister, clean the area with soap and treated water, pop the blister with a sterile needle, and apply antibiotic ointment. Leaving the flap of skin that covers the blister intact will help keep it clean and prevent infection. Cover the blister with a sterile bandage. I like to put an O-shaped foam covering over the blister and secure it with moleskin or duct tape. Periodically clean the blister and rebandage it. If you are in too much pain to continue hiking, find the easiest way out and plan your trip for another time.

Appendix 3 contains a list of items your first-aid kit ought to hold.

Depending on your sensitivities and where you are traveling, you may also want to carry hydrocortisone cream for skin irritations, an antacid, an antihistamine, a decongestant, tweezers for disengaging ticks, and epinephrine if you have an allergy that may cause anaphylaxis.

Weather

Hypothermia

As backpackers, we spend a lot of time choosing waterproof jackets and synthetic layers, waterproofing our boots and our tents, and planning safe routes. During a trip, we go to great lengths to keep a shirt and a pair of socks dry and to keep our sleeping bag from getting soaked in a downpour. We do these things not just for our comfort but for our personal safety. Getting wet and cold, and not having the resources to warm up, can lead to a serious condition called hypothermia. This condition arises when our bodies get so cold that they can't generate enough heat to get warm again. The moment you begin to lose heat faster than you can produce it is the moment you begin to suffer from exposure.

You don't have to be winter camping to get hypothermia; in fact, most hypothermic conditions develop in temperatures between 30° and 50°F. A hypothermic condition is aggravated by rain, wind, and exhaustion, which is why we spend so much time trying to stay dry and comfortable. If a person in your hiking group shows signs of hypothermia—shivering, mumbling, numbness, glassy stare, apathy, loss of consciousness—you need to treat the person immediately. People with hypothermia often may not know they are experiencing a serious condition, even when they are so cold they cannot unwrap a granola bar or zip their jacket. It will often be up to you to recognize the signs and treat the victim.

If you can get to a warmer place (say, off the exposed ridge), do so. Once you're out of the wind or rain, remove any wet clothing from the victim. Warm the person in a sleeping bag, give him or her a warm drink, and build a campfire if possible. Sugary drink mixes will help to jump-start the person's metabolism. If the person will not warm up, climb into the sleeping bag with the victim and use your body heat to keep him or her warm. Whatever you do, don't let the person fall asleep.

Your best defense against hypothermia is to take preventive measures. Bundle up before you get cold and put on the rain gear before the downpour. Eat high-energy foods periodically and stay

When Dry Clothes Can Save Your Life

One night in early spring I was camping at a three-sided log shelter in the southern Appalachians. It was warm that day and the walking was comfortable, but in the late afternoon the wind picked up and the skies looked threatening. The valley was socked in with thick, gray clouds, and you knew it was going to be one of those rains that would last for days. Fortunately I had a rainjacket and a pack fly, so the contents of my pack stayed relatively dry. I couldn't believe how quickly the temperature dropped! As soon as I stopped walking, the wind and rain numbed my fingers. Although I was chilled and shaking when I got to the shelter, I had dry clothes to change into. I crawled into my dry sleeping bag, made a hot cup of tea, and spent the rest of the afternoon watching it rain.

Later that evening, three college students arrived at the shelter. Their sleeping bags were tied with twine to the outside of their packs and the bags weren't in stuff sacks. The bags were drenched. The boys didn't have pack flies so all their gear was wet. They entered the shelter and just stood there, not knowing what to do. It was clear they would become hypothermic if they didn't warm up. A few other campers managed to get a small fire started, and we encouraged the boys to get into their sleeping bags. We helped them get settled and made sure they had food. Although they had a miserable night huddling together in their wet bags, they stayed warm enough to make it through the night. As they left the next morning, they were clearly humbled.

I understand how easy it is to keep hiking during a rain shower and not be concerned about getting wet. After all, you're often warm when you're moving, and the night is a long way off. But after a bad experience, you understand how important it is to take action to stay warm and dry before you start getting wet. It can be terribly frightening when you get so cold that you can't warm up.

hydrated. Always keep dry clothes in your backpack, and do whatever it takes to keep them dry. Run around or do jumping jacks for a minute if you start to feel cold at a rest break. Have a hot drink before you climb into your sleeping bag for the night. On all backpacking trips, it's a good idea to bring a hat and gloves.

Hyperthermia

Hyperthermia is a condition that develops when your body gets so hot it can't cool down. Backpacking in very high temperatures may be dangerous, so it's good to take it slow and look for symptoms of a heat-related illness. The first signs of a heat-related illness are often heat cramps, which are painful muscle spasms that often occur in the legs or abdomen. If you develop heat cramps on a backpacking trip, sit down and drink fluids immediately. If heat cramps go untreated, they may lead to a more serious condition like heat exhaustion.

A person suffering from heat exhaustion may have pale or flushed skin and rapid and shallow breathing. He or she may complain of dizziness, weakness, nausea, and a headache. If someone in your hiking group experiences these symptoms, move him or her to a cooler place (like under a shade tree, or beside a stream) and wipe the person's face with a wet bandanna. Elevate the person's feet and have him or her sip water.

A heat-related illness can be very serious; act quickly to cool the person down as soon as symptoms of a hyperthermic condition are noted. Again, your best defense is prevention. If you're traveling in high temperatures, rest often and drink water frequently. Eat salty food to help restore your electrolyte balance. Drape a wet bandanna over your head and wear proper clothing like a sun hat, sunglasses, and a lightweight, light-colored long-sleeve shirt. Avoid hiking in the middle of the day. Relax during the middle of the day, and hike in the morning and evening.

Lightning

Every year, lightning kills nearly two hundred people and injures about nine hundred in the United States. Traveling at speeds up to 300 miles per second, lightning can hurl a person through the air, cause a person's heart to stop beating, or burn the clothes off his or her back. If a thunderstorm occurs while you're backpacking, you need to make every effort to get out of the path of lightning. If you're on an exposed ridge, get down into a valley as quickly as possible. Don't stand in a meadow or next to a large solitary tree; instead, seek shelter in low-lying areas and scout out dense stands of small trees. Avoid standing on rocks, and don't crawl into a cave for protection.

Avoid bodies of water and anything metal, including your backpack and your tent poles. The metal in the frame of your backpack makes you a walking lightning rod, so if lightning is very close to you, take off your pack and move away from it. If you feel that lightning is striking extremely close to you, move several yards away from your hiking partner and squat down, touching only the soles of your boots to the ground.

ANIMALS

Large Mammals

Backpacking in an area that supports a top predator has a different feel to it than most other backpacking trips. It's humbling to know that in some places you're not at the top of the food chain. I still remember the first time I arrived at a trailhead and saw a sign that read, "Stay Alert! You Are Entering Grizzly Country." There was something terribly exciting and frightening about hiking through an area that is wild enough to support a population of grizzlies. It was a tremendous experience, although I couldn't fully relax on that trip; I was always wondering what I would do if I ran into a bear. It's good to have a healthy fear of large mammals, and when you're traveling through their habitat, you need to be aware of their behaviors and know how to respond should you encounter one. Mountain lions, wolves, alligators, wolverines, and even less-predatory animals such as moose, javelinas, and domesticated cattle can be dangerous if they charge you.

If you are recreating in an area that is home to grizzly bears (in pockets of the northwestern contiguous United States and Alaska), consult local officials to learn how to avoid the bears and how to respond should you see them. Do the same when traveling in mountain lion and wolf country. Becoming educated about the wildlife in your area is the first step toward coexisting peacefully with large predators.

For the sake of space, I won't discuss methods of dealing with every potentially dangerous animal in North America. Instead, I'll focus on the one that we are most likely to encounter on backcountry journeys in the United States: the black bear. In my experiences, black bears have always been more scared of me (which is certainly puzzling, considering their size) and have fled the area the moment they saw me. But every encounter is different, and there's no way to predict how an individual bear will react.

The most important thing you can do is not attract a bear to you. Store food and toiletries away from your tent at night (proper food storage techniques are discussed on pages 72 to 73). Don't bring any scented items—toothpaste, a candy bar, lotion—into the tent with you, and don't eat or cook in or near the tent when you are in bear country.

At camp, it is best to form a triangle with your sleeping area, cooking area, and food storage area. Each point of the triangle should be at least 100 yards from the other two points. Maintain a clean camp by following proper cleaning, cooking, and food storage techniques (these techniques are discussed on pages 71 to 75), and you'll likely have safe travels through bear country.

You can also avoid bears by learning how to recognize bear sign and prints. Local rangers can teach you about bear behavior and show you how to identify bear markings.

Most of the time, a bear will hear you or smell you long before you see it. But sometimes an encounter can't be avoided. You may surprise a bear on the trail or see one in a meadow across the valley. If you do come upon a bear that hasn't seen you, talk loudly to make it aware of your presence; you never want to sneak up on a bear. When it hears you, the bear will usually run away. If it doesn't, back away slowly. The most dangerous situation is when you stand between a mother and her cubs. If you see cubs anywhere, move away from them immediately.

Never turn and run if you see any potentially dangerous animal; running invites a chase, and you cannot outrun a bear. Also, as cumbersome as a bear may appear, you won't be able to outswim one. It is best to appear calm (even if you're not feeling that way) and move slowly. Face the bear and wave your arms over your head so the bear knows you're not another bear. In the unlikely

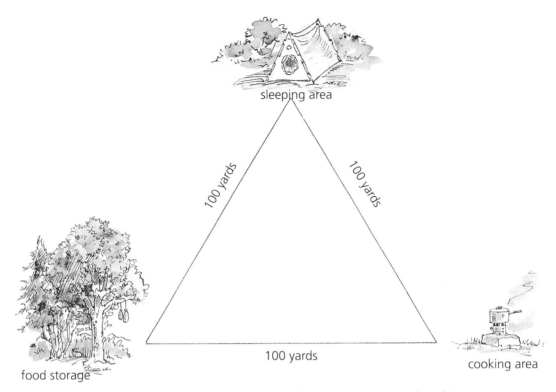

In bear country, form a triangle with your sleeping area, food storage area, and cooking area.

event that the black bear attacks you, fight back with whatever weapons you can find; black bears have been fought off with sticks, rocks, and trekking poles.

If you are traveling through an area home to a large predatory mammal, you may want to carry a canister of pepper spray. Make sure the spray is specifically designed for wildlife attacks; the Mace at your local drug store won't do. One popular brand called Counter Assault is sold at many outfitting and hardware stores for about $40, or you can order it directly from Counter Assault (see appendix 5). It may feel empowering to go backpacking with a can of pepper spray secured on your hipbelt, but don't enter the woods thinking you are invincible. A spray will be your last line of defense, and the success of the spray in deterring an aggressive attack is not guaranteed.

If you're in bear country, however, pepper spray might do you more harm than good: bear biologists have found that pepper spray can actually attract bears, since it's made from food products

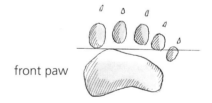

front paw

rear paw

Black bear prints.

(ground-up peppers in vegetable oil). Bears are likely to investigate interesting smells and unfamiliar objects, a description that fits your canister of pepper spray. When I worked as a backcountry ranger in Denali National Park in Alaska, we urged backpackers to store pepper spray with their food, at least 100 yards away from the tent.

One item I urge you to leave at home is a gun. Unless you are hunting, weapons like these have no place in the backpacker's pack. Guns make the backcountry far more dangerous than it should be, and their effectiveness in deterring attacks is questionable—if you shoot at something like a grizzly bear (which, by the way, is illegal in most places unless the bear is in the process of mauling you), you had better make a perfect shot or you're likely to aggravate the bear even further.

Snakes

There are four types of venomous snakes in North America. The rattlesnake is common throughout much of the United States. The cottonmouth, or water moccasin, is found largely in Southeastern swamps. Copperheads can be found in the East, and the coral snake resides in the Southwest and Southeast. Contact a local ranger district to determine whether venomous snakes are in the region through which you will be backpacking.

You'll usually find snakes hiding under rocks and logs. When you're hiking, pay attention to where you place your hands and feet. Most snakebites occur when people unknowingly scare a snake as they reach for a handhold or step into a crevice when traveling through rocky terrain. A sturdy pair of hiking boots and full-length gaiters will provide some protection against snakebites. If you are traveling through snake country, be aware of where you place your hands and feet.

If you are bitten by a venomous snake, there is a chance that the bite is not poisonous because only roughly half of venomous snakebites actually have venom in them. If the bite is poisonous, you may experience a stinging pain, severe burning, nausea, weakness, rapid pulse, and labored breathing. If this is the case, you will need professional medical attention immediately.

If you will be backpacking far from civilization, you may want to carry a Sawyer Venom Extractor kit. Within a minute after being bitten, you can use it to suck out the venom. If you don't have an Extractor kit, don't try to cut the victim or use a tourniquet, and don't apply ice to the wound. If possible, keep the bitten area below the heart, and get the person to a medical facility or bring a doctor to the person as quickly as possible. The Red Cross reports that of the eight thousand people bitten annually in the United States by snakes, the bite is fatal for only about a dozen.

Spiders

There are three types of venomous spiders in the United States. Black widow spiders can be found throughout the country, especially in the East. The brown recluse (a light brown spider with a darker brown, violin-shaped marking on its back) is typically found in the Midwest and parts of the South, while other recluse spiders are found in the Southwest. The Northwest is home to the hobo spider.

Although most of the spiders you'll encounter will be harmless, keep in mind that you are traveling through the spiders' homes and that there's a chance you'll come across a venomous variety. Be aware of any venomous spiders that may reside in the area through which you are backpacking, and avoid places they are likely to reside. Spiders prefer

violin marking on body

Brown recluse spider.

hourglass
marking
on body

Black widow spider.

dark, out-of-the-way places, so be aware of where you place your hands if you're sitting on a rock or fumbling around in an outhouse. A spider is likely to bite if it's provoked or feels trapped.

You will know immediately if you've been bitten. The bite of a black widow spider (a black spider that has a reddish hourglass shape on its underside) may produce severe cramps, nausea, and sweating. The bite of the recluse and hobo spiders produces a lesion on your skin and will give you flulike symptoms. If you've been bitten, don't move the part of your body that's been affected. If the bite occurred on your arm or leg, keep the limb below the level of your heart. Encourage bleeding to get rid of the venom, then apply a cold, wet bandanna to the bite. Get to a doctor immediately, or send someone to bring a doctor to you. It is helpful if you can describe the spider that bit you so your doctor can give you the correct antivenin, which counteracts the poison.

Ticks

In many places throughout the country, ticks can be a problem, especially from May through August. Many people are concerned about contracting Lyme disease from the deer tick or the western black-legged tick. Because deer ticks are so small (they can be as small as a poppy seed), it may be hard to tell if you've been bitten. In fair-skinned people, the bite causes a circular rash with a clear center. The bite can produce fatigue, muscle and joint pain, swollen glands, a sore throat, and a headache. If you experience these symptoms, get to a doctor as soon as you can because Lyme disease can be debilitating if left untreated. Your doctor can prescribe antibiotics that will have you feeling better in no time.

Your best defense against ticks is to check yourself and your hiking partners often. Wearing light-colored pants and shirts will help you spot them. I also like to tuck the bottom of my pants into my socks to prevent a tick from crawling under my pants leg. Be sure to wear a hat or a bandanna as well. If you notice that a tick is biting you, grasp it with tweezers as close to your skin as possible and gently pull it out. Clean the bite immediately. Most bites won't cause you to become sick because many disease-causing bacteria are transmitted only after the tick has been attached to you for hours or even days.

Mosquitoes

Although mosquitoes are dangerous only in rare instances, they can certainly make a backpacking journey unpleasant. If there is a chance that mosquitoes will be in the area in which you are backpacking, bring some sort of bug repellent. Different people have varied success with different brands and potencies; there is no single best formula.

Certainly the most potent formula is DEET (however, don't equate potency with superiority because potent formulas can come with some nasty side effects). If you use DEET, select a concentration below 50 percent. Never apply DEET to children or to your hands, face, or clothing. Also don't use DEET if you're pregnant or nursing. DEET will eat through synthetic materials, so make sure you keep it away from your gear, too. If you feel queasy or experience a headache or hot flashes, discontinue use immediately. As always, never rinse DEET off your body in a water source.

There are a few natural alternatives to using DEET to fend off mosquitoes. Try these techniques. First, do your best to not smell like a fresh human: don't wear any scented products like deodorant, lotion, or perfume. Second, take breaks on open, windy places, like high meadows or ridge tops, where the breezes are likely to keep the mosquitoes at bay. Third, remain calm—swatting and slapping will only encourage them. If the bugs are persistent, try wearing a bug net on your head, and look for bug-proof shirts and pants at your local outdoor store. As a final precaution, toss a tube of anti-itch ointment in your pack, just in case.

Be aware of other potentially dangerous animals that reside in the area through which you are hiking. Learn where they are likely to be found, what they're attracted to, how they can be harmful, and what to do if one is encountered.

PLANTS

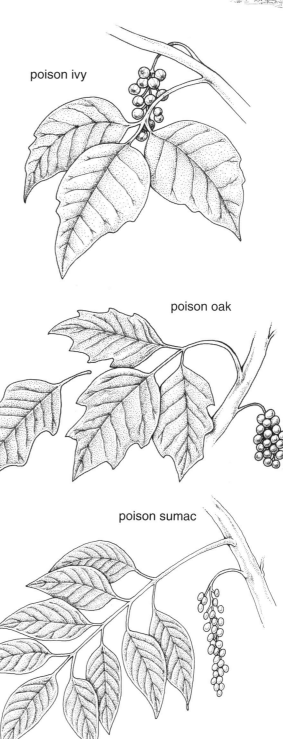

poison ivy

poison oak

poison sumac

Inquire at a ranger station or consult a guidebook about plants in the area that may be dangerous. Local officials can show you pictures of plants to avoid and teach you how to identify them. Study the images so you know exactly which plants to stay away from.

The three poisonous plants you are most likely to encounter on a backpacking trip are poison ivy, poison oak, and poison sumac. If you come into contact with one of these, wash the affected area immediately. If sores develop, lotions such as Calamine or Caladryl may help relieve the pain.

PEOPLE

Certainly you have a greater chance of encountering a hostile individual in a city than you do in the backcountry. Although I consider backpacking an extremely safe activity, every now and then we hear about an attack in the woods. It is important to note, however, that attacks in the backcountry usually occur along trails or in shelters that are within close proximity to a road or a town. If you will be traveling in a densely populated area or following a trail that is easily accessed by a road or a town, take the following precautions to minimize your chances of a violent encounter.

Never tell strangers where you plan to camp or the exact route you plan to follow. Carry a plastic whistle; a series of three blows signals distress. If you would feel more comfortable carrying something that will fend off an attacker, carry Mace or pepper spray in a holster on your hip. You may also feel safer if you travel in a group. Regardless of where you travel, it is always a good idea to leave your itinerary with a friend or at a ranger station. Should something happen to you (an injury, illness, or if you get lost), authorities will know where to look to find you.

Trust your instincts. If someone or something makes you feel uncomfortable, get yourself out of the situation. Whatever you do, don't carry a gun for protection. The last thing we need is for our wilderness to turn into a war zone. You have a better chance of hurting yourself or your hiking partner with your gun than you do of being attacked in the backcountry. You also run the risk of tangling with local regulations about firearms.

The few violent crimes that have been committed in the backcountry usually involve nonhikers; the people you meet deep in the backcountry will almost always be friendly. With regard to other people, you ought to be more concerned about getting in the way of a hunter than about being a victim of a premeditated assault. During hunting season, it can be dangerous to wander through the backcountry. Become informed about the various hunting seasons in the area through which you will travel. If you can, plan your trip to avoid the hunting season.

If you do go backpacking during hunting season, know what is being hunted and avoid areas where that animal is likely to be present. Stay on the trail and make hunters aware of your presence by creating noise as you walk (talking or singing works well). If you're in or adjacent to an area where hunting is permitted, outfit yourself in blaze orange. Tie an orange vest to your backpack, and if you have a dog, make him or her wear one, too.

EXPANDING YOUR HORIZONS

With experience, you will become proficient in a variety of backpacking skills, and you'll feel more and more comfortable in the woods. After a while, you'll be ready to diversify your experience or seek backpacking adventures beyond weekend jaunts in your local park. Challenging yourself with longer trips, with varied terrain, or by adding children or pets to your hiking party is a good way to broaden your experiences in the backcountry. With each new challenge, you will have the opportunity to set new goals and push your limits. With each new adventure comes the opportunity to grow, to achieve, and to create memories that will last a lifetime.

LONGER TRIPS

It is quite possible that after only a few backpacking trips you will want to stay out longer, go deeper, and cover more miles. Sometimes the most difficult part of a trip is turning around and heading home. There always seems to be just one more lake you want to visit or one more mountain you want to climb. I admit I'm an adventure addict. You may be, too. If you find yourself inflicted with the backpacking bug, you may want to consider planning a long trip. I consider a trip of two or three weeks to be a long trip.

It often takes more than a few days to get into the rhythm of walking every day and to fully absorb your surroundings. Living in the woods for extended periods allows you to settle into the backpacking routine, gives you a heightened sense of awareness, and makes it possible for you to connect with the landscape and with yourself in ways you may never have thought were possible.

If you think you would like to try long-distance backpacking, the following steps will get you off on the right foot.

Pick a Trail

Opportunities abound for long-distance trekking. For starters, consider one of our national scenic trails. In 1968 the National Trails System Act was passed, which established the Appalachian Trail (2,159 miles from Georgia to Maine) and the Pacific Crest Trail (2,600 miles from Mexico to Canada) as the country's first national scenic trails, and it set the stage for six other long trails that have been added over the years. These include the Continental Divide Trail (3,200 miles from Mexico to Canada); Florida Trail (1,300 miles from Big Cypress National Preserve to the western panhandle); Ice Age Trail (1,000 miles from Lake Michigan to the Saint Croix River along the Minnesota–Wisconsin border); Natchez Trace Trail (110 miles from Natchez, Mississippi, to Nashville, Tennessee); North Country Trail (expected to be 4,600 miles from the Adirondack Mountains, New York, to the Missouri River in South Dakota); and Potomac Heritage Trail (700 miles through Virginia, Maryland, District of Columbia, and Pennsylvania). (Contact information for trail conferences that oversee our nation's national scenic trails is listed in appendix 5.)

You can also contact the American Hiking Society for information on other long-distance trails that are not nationally recognized. (Contact information for national hiking organizations is listed in appendix 5.) Some of the more popular trails include the Long Trail (from Vermont to Canada), the John Muir Trail (in California), and the American Discovery Trail (from the Atlantic coast to the Pacific coast). Canada has a number of long trails, and long treks in Europe and Asia are becoming increasingly more popular.

Of the national scenic trails, the Appalachian Trail is the most popular, with two-thirds of the American population living within a day's drive of it. The Appalachian Trail attracts nearly 4 million visitors each year, and every year about 2,000 people attempt to hike the trail in its entirety. An end-to-end hike generally takes about six months.

But long-distance trails don't need to be hiked from end to end. Choose whichever area appeals to you, and work within your time constraints and your physical abilities. Always keep your goals in sight, and choose part of a long trail that's right for you.

Choose a Season

Travel during a time of the year that will allow you to have the best possible experience. Deep snows often linger on mountain passes until June, and at high elevations, snow falls as early as September. Desert travel may be inappropriate in the height of summer. Certain parks or trails may be closed during different seasons to protect wildlife or to prevent overuse during popular recreation periods. Determine the best time of year to hike the trail you've selected.

Determine Time and Distance

Many people have limited vacation time or limited opportunities to leave their normal life. How much time you have to backpack will help you determine how many miles you can realistically cover.

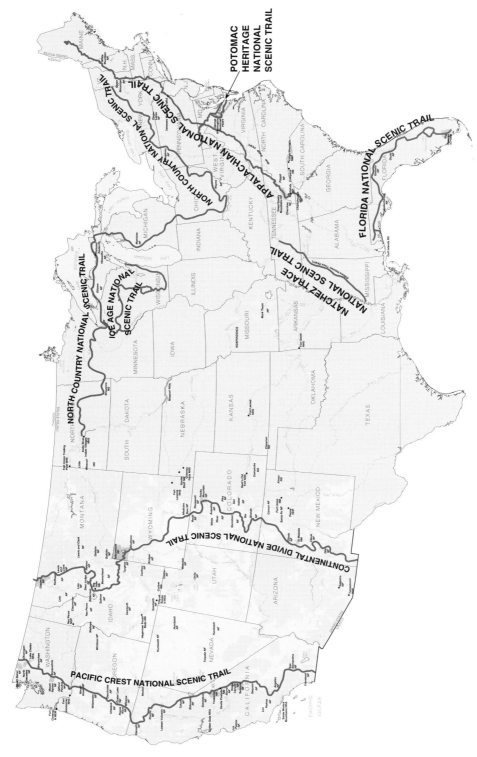

POTOMAC HERITAGE NATIONAL SCENIC TRAIL

APPALACHIAN NATIONAL SCENIC TRAIL

NORTH COUNTRY NATIONAL SCENIC TRAIL

ICE AGE NATIONAL SCENIC TRAIL

NORTH COUNTRY NATIONAL SCENIC TRAIL

FLORIDA NATIONAL SCENIC TRAIL

NATCHEZ TRACE NATIONAL SCENIC TRAIL

CONTINENTAL DIVIDE NATIONAL SCENIC TRAIL

PACIFIC CREST NATIONAL SCENIC TRAIL

Backpacking opportunities abound along our nation's eight National Scenic trails.

Contact the Trail Association for Information

You can find information about your trail from the organization that oversees its construction and maintenance. Sometimes that will be a federal agency like the U.S. Forest Service or the National Park Service. Many times a more localized group assumes management responsibilities for the trail (contact information for trail conferences can be found in appendix 5). Many of these organizations can sell you guidebooks or publications that will help you plan a long trip. I suggest reading the trail's guidebook if you plan to embark on a longer trip.

One of the best ways to learn more about long-distance backpacking is to talk with someone who has completed a longer trip. You will find experienced backpackers at trail club meetings or at trail maintenance and trail construction events. Volunteering for trail work is one of the best ways to get involved. There is something tremendously rewarding about being part of a team that builds a trail through the woods. When you walk that section of trail, you will think of it as your own. Consider your efforts payback for all the trail miles you've walked or hope to walk. Some of us believe that doing trail work is also good karma for your upcoming adventure!

Trail work will not only give you an appreciation for trails, but it also will put you in contact with avid hikers. If you are considering a long-distance trek, contact the association that directs management for that trail, and ask how you can help. Talk to other volunteers about the route and about your plans. They may be able to give you valuable advice for your upcoming trek.

Consider How You Will Resupply

Because you cannot carry all your food and supplies for an entire long-distance hike, you will have to periodically replenish your supplies. The easiest way to resupply is to send yourself care packages filled with food and gear. Oftentimes, general stores in rural areas accept packages so you won't have to venture to a post office in a large town. Guidebooks for popular long-distance trails contain detailed descriptions of post offices and general stores along your route. Before your trip, divide the length of the journey into sections of trail that will take about five days to hike. Bring food for the first five days, then package food for the next five days in a box. Address the box to yourself, and label the box "General Delivery." Consult a guidebook or veteran hiker to find out how to get to the post office from the trail. Your box should contain food for the number of days it will take you to hike to your next mail drop.

For longer trips, diversify your food to avoid getting bored with recurring meals of oatmeal and pasta. Throw a treat or two into each box as a reward. Toss in a fresh pair of socks, extra film, supplies to replenish your first-aid kit, additional iodine tablets, or gear to suit changing weather conditions. For example, if you expect the weather conditions to get cooler during your journey, send yourself warmer clothing.

Know the hours and days the post office is open and call ahead of time to determine how long it will hold a box for a hiker. Most post offices will hold a box for a few months, but it's good to make sure. It's often helpful to write your estimated date of arrival on the box and label the box "Hiker Box" so the postal workers know that your schedule is likely to change.

In addition to food and gear, you will also need to buy fuel along the way. Call hardware, grocery, or outfitting stores along your proposed route to make sure they carry the right kind of fuel. Most trail towns sell white gas and some sort of canister fuel. Use auto fuel (lowest octane available) only as a last resort.

If you'd rather not mess with mail drops, you will be able to find basic food items in towns near the trail. But keep in mind that small grocers may not have the best supply of backpacking food, and shopping at small stores is more expensive than buying your food in bulk at discounted prices before you leave.

Occasionally hikers like to stash food and supplies along the trail ahead of time. Caching your food can be risky—you need to make sure that you can find the stashed food and that you get to it before an animal does. Caching supplies can save time during the hike because you won't need to divert from the trail to claim a mail drop. If your goal is to avoid civilization, caching supplies can be a good technique.

A final thought about long trips. Long-distance backpacking is different from weekend or week-long trips because backpacking becomes not just a recreational activity but a way of life. When you spend a long time moving at a slow pace, you begin to change. You get perspective. You reduce your needs to basic ones: eating, staying warm and dry, finding water, finding shelter. Walking through a specific region of the country is a great way to get to know the area and to meet the people who reside there. It can certainly be a wonderful way to live.

Why We Do It

I can talk for hours about the dozens of hardships I've encountered on long-distance hikes. I have stories of blinding blizzards, chronic blisters, assaults by blackflies and mosquitoes, aching muscles, throbbing knees, dangerous river crossings. But there's something about taking long walks that makes me want to keep doing it. Sometimes I think it's the challenge, that I have to prove something to myself. Sometimes I think I do it to explore a region of the country, to pass by slowly and take time to absorb the landscape and the people. I certainly feel like I've gotten to know the places through which I've walked.

But mostly I think I'm attracted to the lifestyle of a long-distance hiker, the way the trail strips you down and builds someone stronger. During a long hike, I feel healthy and present and in tune with myself. It's easy to neglect these things in society, but on the trail your needs are simplified, your attention is focused, and distractions are minimal. You are forced to look inside yourself, dig deep, and find a part of yourself that may have gotten pushed aside in civilization. I have yet to meet a long-distance hiker who didn't come out of the woods liking the person that he or she discovered. We hikers try to bring the focus and confidence of that person back with us. We hold on to it for as long as we can until we begin to fray around the edges. Then we find a guidebook and pack our bags, and set out again to reclaim something we think we lost.

ADVANCED TERRAIN

The environment in which you hike can provide diverse and exciting opportunities to test your skills and sense of adventure. Terrain, weather, and altitude will affect your experiences and comfort level in the backcountry. Of course, what is perceived as difficult for one person may be commonplace for another. For example, if you grew up in the High Sierras and are in superb physical condition, a steep, high-altitude trek won't feel as difficult as it will to a person coming from sea level. The great part about backpacking is that you can choose the terrain, altitude, and season of your trip (which will influence the weather you will be likely to encounter). In a sense, by selecting the environment through which you'll travel, you will be handpicking your own challenges.

As you know, backpacking terrain ranges from flat gravel paths to steep technical climbs. Expand your horizons by planning a hike on terrain that you are unaccustomed to. For those who have an affinity for climbing mountains, you may want to learn some mountaineering skills and test your limits on more advanced climbs. Mountaineering ascents often involve technical climbing and glacier and crevasse travel, which requires additional gear like crampons, climbing rope, and ice axes. (See appendix 5 for books on mountaineering.)

A trip can also be made more challenging if you visit a region you are unaccustomed to. Most people in the United States live in low-elevation, forested regions, so a trip to the desert or to an alpine area may provide greater challenge and broader experiences.

Desert Travels

If you are unfamiliar with desert environments, you will be enthralled by the unusual plant and animal life, and by the striking rock formations, of many arid regions. Weather is typically hot and dry, so

If you're unfamiliar with arid climes, broaden your horizons on a desert backpacking trip.

you won't need to carry a heavy tent or bulky clothes. You will, however, need to carry more water. On a desert backpacking trip, water and shade become your biggest concerns. In 100-degree temperatures, hikers ought to consume at least 2 gallons of water per day. Inquire ahead of time about the availability of water; sometimes you may have to carry water for a day or two at a time. Consult guidebooks specific to the desert region through which you'll be traveling to learn more about water requirements and challenges in that region.

Shade may also be hard to come by, which is why sunscreen and protective clothing are essential. Sunglasses, a sun hat, and light-colored, lightweight, long-sleeve shirts and pants are essential items for the desert traveler. Techniques of desert travel often don't follow the traditional rules of backpacking. For example, a sturdy hiking boot is not necessary; many experienced backpackers feel that a light trail-running shoe is all you need. Also, in hot, arid climes it's OK to wear cotton. In fact, it is often preferable because wet cotton will keep you cool. Bring a bandanna to drape over your head and soak it in cool water every chance you get. (For more information on desert backpacking, see the books listed in appendix 5.)

Alpine Adventures

On the opposite end of the spectrum is alpine backpacking. Alpine environments are those areas that are above the elevation where trees can grow. In alpine environments, we say that we are above "tree line." On such trips you will be most concerned about staying warm and dry, so your clothing is likely to be bulky and your tent able to withstand high winds, low temperatures, snow, and hail. Weather can change within minutes; a thunderstorm can seemingly come out of nowhere, and it can vanish as quickly as it came. The views on an alpine excursion are often unparalleled because they are unobstructed by trees. Walking through alpine meadows with wildflowers up to your waist is just one of the many joys you are likely to find on high-mountain treks.

Opportunities for adventure abound in alpine environments.

In alpine environments, altitude is likely to affect your experience. No one knows why some people acclimatize better to high elevations than others. Current thought is that it has little to do with physical fitness and more to do with how much time you spend letting your body adjust to higher elevations. If you will be traveling to an elevation above 8,000 feet, or much higher than you're accustomed to, plan to ascend gradually and spend a night or two before the trip acclimatizing.

Altitude sickness, also called acute mountain sickness, is a common problem among hikers who venture to lofty regions. Symptoms of altitude sickness include shortness of breath, headache, fatigue, loss of appetite, and dizziness. If your condition worsens and the symptoms become uncomfortable, get to a lower elevation as quickly as possible.

Winter Camping

The time of year in which you travel will also affect your experiences in the backcountry. Although most people go backpacking exclusively in the summer, there are advantages to going in the winter. Solitude and a feeling of detachment from civilization are easier to come by. You can avoid the crowds at popular destinations, and you won't have to worry about those pesky mosquitoes! If you regularly travel to a particular destination in the summer, it may be fun to experience it in a different light; it may give you a new perspective on an area that has come to feel commonplace.

Winter camping comes with a handful of caveats, however. First, you need to be concerned about staying warm and dry, so proper layering and gear choices are essential. You will need a

Challenge yourself with winter camping.

Sleeping in Snow

When a friend of mine insisted that winter camping would be a fun endeavor, you could say I was skeptical. She told me how she had wanted to build a snow cave for years but could never find anyone to go with her. That dozens of her other friends thought it was a bad idea was not reassuring. Reluctantly I said I would give it a shot.

We skied about a mile from the car and began digging. At first it was fun; it was a beautiful day, quiet and sparkling. We traced deer tracks across a meadow and saw a snowshoe hare. Beaded mouse prints strung across the snow from bush to bush. The snowdrift we chose for our cave was too shallow, and we abandoned it after an hour of shoveling. It actually took three collapsed caves and a day of shoveling to get it right. We learned that we had to pile snow, let it sit and harden for a while, then hollow it out. Exhausted and frustrated, we kept digging, determined to spend the night in a decent shelter. Our final effort was a work of art—at least *we* thought so. And that was all that mattered. We constructed a cave with room for two sleeping bags and room at our feet to store extra gear. The entrance was small and slightly lower than the sleeping space so heat wouldn't escape out the top.

We organized our gear and carved little shelves into the wall of the cave. One small candle illuminated the entire space, and as I snuggled into my sleeping bag, it actually felt cozy. I felt nestled in the earth and had the sense of being encased in a white, glowing womb.

That night I was afraid that the cave would collapse and I would be buried under 4 feet of snow. I slept on and off, willing myself to accept whatever fate was to come. As it turned out, the cave held throughout the night and probably lasted until spring when the snow melted. When we packed our gear the next morning, I turned to my friend and said, "You know, we should definitely do this again."

four-season tent to withstand more severe weather conditions, and you may need snowshoes or skis to traverse snowy areas. You must find a stove that will work in very cold conditions, and you must keep your boots and water from freezing during the night. For added adventure, learn how to build a snowcave, dig a fire pit for cooking, and test for avalanche conditions. These advanced techniques are sure to heighten your backpacking experiences (to learn more about winter camping, refer to the books listed in appendix 5).

Opportunities to diversify your travels abound in the backcountry. Whether you choose to climb peaks over 14,000 feet, pick your way through the Everglades, or explore a narrow canyon in southern Utah, without a doubt, your trip will be an adventure.

BACKPACKING WITH CHILDREN

If you thought backpacking was an adult activity, think again. Sharing with children the joys of backpacking can be a very rewarding experience. Their enthusiasm for the outdoors will be reflected in their eyes, their questions, and their smiles. Exposing children to wild places and to outdoor activities can have a profound impact on their development and life choices. Children who are introduced to the backcountry at a young age tend to be more comfortable and confident in the outdoors when they get older.

My parents took me camping every summer when I was growing up in Pennsylvania. Although we were always close to urban areas, it felt like the deepest, darkest wilderness to me and my younger brother. Early camping trips heightened my interest in ecology and natural history, subjects that I pursued in college. These early experiences gave me the confidence to try other outdoor activities and pursue longer backpacking trips. Today, outdoor

adventure has become my passion and livelihood. Who knows? Backpacking trips could have a similar effect on a child of your own.

Most parents feel that backpacking with their children is as rewarding for them as it is for the little ones. Backpacking is something the entire family can do, and with so many distractions in urban society, it's nice to spend quality time with your family in a setting that fosters communication and personal discovery. The backcountry also provides unlimited entertainment for children, so as parents, you won't need to constantly entertain your troupe.

As it is with most things in life, the rewards don't come without a challenge. And backpacking with children has its own set of challenges. This section will provide you with information to help you overcome many of these challenges and to make your family outings as smooth as possible. (For further reading on family camping, refer to the books listed in appendix 5.)

Backpacking with children can be a great way to spend quality time with family and friends.

Give your children some say in planning the trip. Show them the map and the trail and give them options. Ask if they would like to camp by the lake or in the meadow. Do they want to take the up-and-back trail or the loop trail? Give them some ownership of the trip. Choose a destination that they will look forward to. A tangible destination like a shelter or a lake is always a good choice. Choose a route that everyone in your group can manage. The goal with children is often not to climb big peaks or set record mileage; being out there is often enough. The idea is not to exhaust you, your children, or your sense of humor, but to choose terrain and a season that will allow you to have an enjoyable and comfortable walk. Often a few miles on gentle terrain will provide a memorable experience. Children will not be interested in walking long distances; they'll be happier playing at camp, so if a half mile or a mile gets them to a place that feels "out there," then that will be good enough. Plan to travel about a half mile per hour.

Build excitement for the trip by having your children help you set up the tent in the backyard. Let them sleep in the backyard so they get accustomed to the tent and to nighttime sounds. Let them wear their hiking shoes to school. Allow them to help you plan and prepare food for the trip. Pack their favorite food items and let them know which items are treats on backpacking trips.

Start small. Hike a couple of miles and spend one night in the woods. That may be enough for you and the children. As you become more experienced and as your children get used to backpacking, you may want to extend your trips. I know couples who spend weeks at a time backpacking with children. After a while, you and your children will find a comfortable routine, and parents tell me there's no better way to spend a family vacation.

One word of caution: backpacking with infants is different from backpacking with toddlers or older children. Before you take an infant into the backcountry, you ought to be comfortable with your own backpacking routine. Once you've had experience setting up camp, cooking meals, finding routes, and camping in inclement weather, you may be ready for the responsibility of sharing your adventures with an infant.

Infants and Young Children

Child carriers ($150) are backpacks made for carrying infants or small children. The packs are designed to carry children who weigh up to 40 or 50 pounds. After that, the children ought to be able to walk on their own. Child carriers usually have a storage pouch beneath the child's seat for stowing diapers, snacks, toys, and other items.

Use a child carrier to transport babies and small children.

When you hike with a child who must be carried, it is helpful to travel with a few other adults. Because one of you will carry the infant, the other adults must carry the infant-toter's gear as well as their own. If you travel with just one other adult, plan to travel more slowly and cover fewer miles than you normally would.

Toddlers and Older Children

If you hike with toddlers or older children, have them carry a pack of their own. A daypack (such as the ones discussed on pages 13 to 14) is appropriate. Until they can carry more weight, they won't need a backpack with a frame. A school pack with padded back and shoulder straps will do.

As your children get older and are able to carry heavier packs, look for child-sized frame packs. Many manufacturers offer smaller frame packs (both internal and external frames) for children (ages seven to twelve). Once they are in junior high school, they may need an adult backpack similar to your own. Have younger children carry 10 percent to 15 percent of their body weight. Let older children pack their own packs, then weigh the packs to make sure they won't be carrying more than one-fourth of their body weight.

Explain to your children how important it is to always carry food, water, and gear that will keep them warm and dry. Make sure they always have snacks, water, and a jacket in their daypacks. As they get older, make them responsible for essential

Hiking trips provide unlimited opportunities for children.

items like their sleeping bag and clothing. Giving them responsibility for the trip will make them feel more included. They are likely to get more out of the trip if they're not just being dragged along.

EQUIPMENT

Infants and Young Children

Most important, you will need to bring a tent large enough to accommodate the entire family, with room to store gear or play a card game. A large tent will be especially useful if you have an infant and need to nurse or comfort the baby in the middle of the night.

Infants and small children don't need their own sleeping bags (the extra bulk of a large bag is not worth carrying, and it will be difficult for a child to warm up a bag that is mostly empty), but they will need their own sleeping space. Cut a foam pad to fit your child and wrap the infant in clothes and baby blankets. Infants can also sleep in full body jumpers. Make sure everyone has a hat.

Toddlers and Older Children

Your children's footwear may be the most important piece of gear they'll have. If your children's feet hurt, you won't hear the end of it! Most of the time, children can wear their sneakers. If the terrain is rocky or if your children are older, you may want to buy them boots with thick soles and ankle support. Most important, their boots or sneakers should be broken in well before their first hiking trip.

Work on blister prevention: have your children wear synthetic liner socks under a heavier wool sock (as you do). Beef up your first-aid kit with plenty of moleskin, and tell your children to stop if they feel a hot spot. Attend to foot problems sooner rather than later.

You may want to sew a child-sized sleeping bag yourself because most children's bags won't be much smaller than your own. If your children will be using large sleeping bags, fold half the bag underneath itself to make the sleeping space smaller.

ON THE TRAIL

Infants and Young Children

Keep babies bundled when they're in the child carrier. Remember that they are not exerting energy the way you are, so they might get cold quickly. Periodically feel a baby's skin, and depending on the conditions, keep a warm hat or a sun hat on him or her at all times.

During rest breaks, be aware of things, such as cactus or poison ivy, that are hazards to a crawling child. Make sure your baby stays hydrated by stopping often for drinks and snacks.

When you bring a baby, you will have to pack out used diapers. You may want to bring cloth diapers because they are light and compact and can be reused. Carry a large supply because diapers can be a challenge to wash on the trail. Never wash diapers directly in a water source. Instead, turn a resealable plastic bag into a washing machine and then discard the waste water 200 feet from the source. Air-dry wet cloth diapers (clean or dirty) to make your load a bit lighter.

Toddlers and Older Children

Have your children carry a plastic whistle at all times. Fasten it with string to their backpacks, and teach them to blow it three times in an emergency. Many parents allow older children to separate from the group as long as they go with a sibling or friend. The buddy system works well. Some parents have children carry an index card in their pack that lists their age, medical needs, phone number, and trip itinerary.

Most likely, your children won't have a problem occupying themselves. However, games can help fill slow times and encourage learning while you walk. Try a scavenger hunt. You can hunt for things without collecting them by having your children spot a squirrel or tell you what a ponderosa pine tree smells like. Bring cards and small, lightweight toys to use inside the tent. Reading a favorite book is always a nice way to end the evening. Have older children keep a journal or make sketches in a small sketch book.

When I was eleven, my mother took me and my brother on a thirty-three-day trip across the United States. Every night, as she was preparing dinner, my brother and I had to write in our journals. It was a great way to reflect on the day and absorb all that we had seen. Today, that journal is one of my most treasured possessions.

Instilling in children an appreciation of the outdoors involves teaching them to respect the environment. Let children know they are in the animals' home, so they ought to act as though they are at a friend's house. Let children know about dangerous animals in the area, and teach them how to respond if they see a bear. Don't let your kids torture animals, and set a good example by not feeding wildlife.

At camp, assign chores for everyone. Have your children help pitch the tent, help prepare the meal, arrange bedding, store food, wash dishes, and fetch water. Plan on taking a long time to settle in at night and to get going in the morning. If you are camped near other hikers, be aware of those who might be searching for solitude. More than ever, your flexibility and good sense of humor will come in handy when backpacking with children.

TAKING THE DOG

Deciding whether to bring your dog on a backpacking trip can be difficult. Some trips are appropriate for dogs; others are not.

Your first obligation is to abide by the laws of the land. Dogs are prohibited from many public lands, like national parks. Check with the managing agency to determine whether dogs are welcome in the area through which you would like to travel. If they aren't, you will need to leave the dog at home or plan to hike somewhere else.

It is generally not a good idea to backpack with a dog that is not under voice control. Dogs in the backcountry must be well behaved, and they must be willing to quickly respond to their owner when called. Set free, your dog may scare other hikers (especially small children), disrupt other camps, and chase wildlife. Most areas require that dogs be leashed at all times. If holding a leash while you backpack will inconvenience you, you may want to reconsider bringing along your dog.

Finally, don't bring a dog when conditions may not be safe for the animal. Evaluate potential hazards such as inclement weather, sharp rocks, extreme heat, ticks, and hunters, and determine whether the journey will be safe for the dog. Also make sure your dog is in shape for backpacking.

Go on a number of long day hikes and monitor your dog's condition. Overweight dogs are predisposed to injury, exhaustion, and heat stroke.

If your dog is in good physical condition and is well behaved, if you'll be backpacking in an area that welcomes pets, and if you are willing to be responsible for your dog's actions, bringing a dog can be an enjoyable experience. I have hiked with an Alaskan malamute on dozens of backcountry excursions, including 500 continuous miles of the Appalachian Trail and over 200 miles of the Colorado Trail. Bringing a pet can be an enormous challenge and a big responsibility, but pets can also be good trail companions and keep you entertained for days.

It's best to visit a veterinarian if you're considering hiking with a dog. Your vet can help you determine whether your dog is in a condition to handle the trip, and he or she can make sure your dog has the proper vaccinations for safe travels.

Equipment

Your dog will require some additional gear. Most owners prefer that their dogs carry their own food. This seems only fair. Many companies man-

Dog Dilemmas

It can be a different experience with a dog. When I added Kodiak, my Alaskan malamute, to my hiking party on the Appalachian Trail, it definitely changed the trip. No longer could I lose myself to the meditative hiking trance. I would snap out of it in a panic, wondering if Kodiak was still behaving himself. In high-use areas, my partner and I always leashed him. It was somewhat of a challenge to hike all day holding on to a leash.

Kodiak sniffed out trouble wherever he could find it. Right off the bat he pounced on a skunk. He couldn't understand why I shrieked and shooed him away when he wanted to snuggle. Later he tried the same tactics with a porcupine and ended up with a nose full of quills.

Still, we were constantly amused by him, by his curiosity of anything that moved, by the way he would nudge his nose through the tent door to see if there was room, by the way he fell to the ground at the end of the day and gave us a scornful look that said, "We *better* be stopping here." He had a way of making us laugh, and it was fun to watch him have such a great time. Although he caused us a good deal of grief, frequent trips to the vet,

and medical bills, we never regretted bringing him along.

We did reach a point, however, where we felt as though we weren't being responsible dog owners. It was easier to let him run free than it was to restrain him on a leash. We felt bad when he chased wildlife and got frustrated when he wouldn't respond to our calls. After one month of hiking with him, we sent him to a friend's house. We learned that it's a lot of work to bring a dog, and it's a big responsibility to make sure the dog is safe and out of trouble.

ufacture saddlebags, which consist of two bags that rest on the dog's sides. The bags are secured by a strap that goes around the dog's chest and another that clasps under the dog's belly.

Your next challenge will be to determine a weight that is appropriate for your dog to carry. I once had a dog that weighed 100 pounds and could comfortably carry a 25-pound load. On longer trips, most of his load consisted of food, so his pack weight became incrementally lighter as the trip progressed and he ate more food. On weekend trips, his pack rarely weighed more than 10 pounds, unless he was especially rambunctious and needed to be slowed down with more weight! A good target pack weight for your dog is 20 percent of his or her body weight; however, be aware of any health conditions your pet might have. If your dog has hip or joint problems, a lighter load may work better.

If you decide to add your gear to your dog's pack, choose items that are not essential to your survival, like sandals or an extra pot, should the dog run off and lose his or her pack. Also choose items that can withstand a beating—your gear may occasionally get slammed into a tree or dragged through a stream.

Your dog will probably be confused the first time you make him or her wear a pack, but dogs seem to adjust quickly to the arrangement and are so excited to go for a walk that they soon forget about their saddlebags.

Because saddlebags are typically water resistant but not

Dog with saddlebags.

Leash your canine companion, especially in heavily used areas or where regulations require it.

waterproof, I recommend storing dog food in double resealable plastic bags before you stow it in the dog's pack. These bags will keep the food dry when your dog decides to go for a spontaneous swim!

Although your everyday leash will probably suffice on the trail, you may opt for something more durable on a backcountry trip. I like to use a climbing rope and carabiner to leash a dog. Buy a piece of climbing rope from an outfitting store (choose whichever thickness and length you desire). Tie a small knot on one end, slip a small carabiner through the knot, and fasten the carabiner to the dog's collar. Tie a larger loop on the other end of the rope to use as a handle. Or, if you have another carabiner, clip the rope to your backpack to free up your hands. Climbing equipment is very durable; climbing rope won't easily fray or tear, and it's difficult for a dog to chew through. My dog's backpacking leash was so efficient it quickly replaced his everyday leash.

When you get to camp, it's a good idea to tie up the dog. I bring about 30 feet of parachute cord for this purpose. That way, the dog has freedom to wander but won't take off after wildlife, and you won't have to worry about him or her while you're going about your camp chores.

Your pooch will also need a food and water bowl. Some manufacturers sell collapsible dog bowls, or you can use your own. Plastic bowls work well. Anything lightweight and durable will do. Make sure you bring both a food and a water bowl because it's not good trail etiquette to let your dog splash around in a water source.

Where to store your dog's gear? In your dog's pack. On longer trips, I also have my dog carry a dog brush and aspirin for aches and pains. As always, make sure your dog wears proper identification and a rabies tag. I also slip a laminated card with the same information into one of the saddlebags, just in case my dog should lose his collar or identification tags.

Etiquette

As a responsible dog owner, you should have your pet under control at all times. If there are other hikers in the area, or if local regulations require it, keep your dog on a leash. Other people may not love your dog as much as you do, and children may

be frightened by dogs. It's a good idea to have your dog wear a muzzle or bring one if you think you'll be recreating in a popular area.

Keep your dog away from other camps and away from the water source. Other hikers may be offended if you let your dog muddy the only water source. Minimum-impact camping skills apply to your dog as well. Bury your dog's fecal matter in a 4- to 8-inch hole. On shorter trips, bring a few extra pouches and pack out your dog's waste, especially if he or she defecates near a water source. If you have a dog that barks a lot, don't camp within earshot of other campers.

Safe Travels for Your Dog

As we mentioned, it's a good idea to tie the dog to a tree or a picnic table when you get to camp. Keeping the dog nearby is as much for the well-being of wildlife as it is for your dog. If your dog goes after an animal like a bear or mountain lion, he or she may not come back. If your dog chases a skunk or porcupine, you'll have a mess on your hands. I've dealt with both, and let me tell you, it's best to avoid the encounter from the get-go.

Be aware of other natural hazards. Fleas, ticks, and parasites like tapeworms are common problems for trail dogs. Check your dog daily for ticks and fleas, and notice any behavioral changes in your pet.

Monitor your dog's progress and check his or her pads regularly. If a dog is unaccustomed to traveling many miles or if the ground is hard or rocky, the dog's pads may get cut or worn down. Pet stores often sell little booties for your pooch that can help protect his or her pads.

Make sure your dog drinks enough water and rests frequently during warm-weather trips. Conversely, make sure your dog stays warm on cold-weather trips. Many hikers let their dogs sleep in the tent vestibule, where they'll stay warm and dry in inclement weather.

Finally, be aware of hunters. If you are traveling through an area during hunting season, I recommend leaving your dog at home. If you do bring your dog, keep him or her on a leash and put an orange vest over the dog's saddlebags. (For more information about trekking with your pooch, refer to the books in appendix 5.)

APPENDIX 1

EQUIPMENT CHECKLIST FOR A DAY HIKE

- ☐ lightweight hiking boots
- ☐ daypack
- ☐ appropriate clothing (not cotton)
- ☐ rainjacket
- ☐ water
- ☐ snacks
- ☐ map
- ☐ compass
- ☐ first-aid kit (to treat blisters, minor cuts, and twists)
- ☐ iodine tablets
- ☐ sunscreen
- ☐ lip balm
- ☐ sunglasses
- ☐ field guides
- ☐ binoculars
- ☐ camera
- ☐ notebook and pen
- ☐ ankle gaiters
- ☐ umbrella

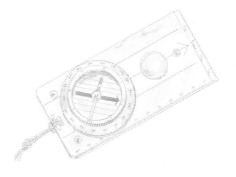

APPENDIX 2

EQUIPMENT CHECKLIST FOR BACKPACKING

Basic Gear

- ❑ backpack with fly
- ❑ hiking boots
- ❑ gaiters
- ❑ tent with rainfly and ground cloth
- ❑ sleeping bag
- ❑ sleeping mattress
- ❑ map and compass
- ❑ water bottle
- ❑ water bag
- ❑ flashlight or headlamp
- ❑ pocketknife or multitool
- ❑ first-aid kit (see details in appendix 3)
- ❑ identification

Clothing

- ❑ hiking socks and liners
- ❑ camp shoes (sandals or sneakers)
- ❑ underwear (sports bra for women)
- ❑ long underwear
- ❑ shorts or hiking pants
- ❑ shirt for hiking
- ❑ shirt for bed
- ❑ rain pants and rainjacket
- ❑ hat
- ❑ gloves
- ❑ bandanna

Kitchenware

- ❑ water purification
- ❑ stove with fuel and windscreen
- ❑ lighter or waterproof matches
- ❑ mug
- ❑ pot with lid
- ❑ pot gripper
- ❑ spoon
- ❑ biodegradable soap and sponge
- ❑ food

Toiletries

- ❑ toothbrush
- ❑ toothpaste
- ❑ comb
- ❑ sunscreen
- ❑ lip balm with sun protection
- ❑ bandanna or pack towel
- ❑ toilet paper and resealable plastic bag for used toilet paper
- ❑ for women: tampons, pads, moist wipes, and extra resealable plastic bags

Other Items

- ❑ sunglasses
- ❑ sun hat
- ❑ bug repellent
- ❑ mesh head net
- ❑ trekking poles
- ❑ tarp
- ❑ watch
- ❑ camera
- ❑ small book
- ❑ guidebook
- ❑ journal and writing implement
- ❑ cards or games
- ❑ pepper spray
- ❑ parachute cord
- ❑ trowel
- ❑ umbrella
- ❑ repair kit (patches, ripstop nylon tape, thread and needle, safety pins)
- ❑ money

APPENDIX 3

- ❏ antibiotic ointment
- ❏ sterile gauze dressings
- ❏ roller bandage
- ❏ triangular bandage
- ❏ 10-cubic-centimeter irrigation syringe with 18-gauge catheter tip for flushing cuts
- ❏ duct tape
- ❏ needle
- ❏ moleskin or other dressing to treat blisters
- ❏ nonaspirin pain reliever
- ❏ elastic bandage
- ❏ Band-Aids
- ❏ first-aid booklet

You may also want to bring

- ❏ hydrocortisone cream
- ❏ antacids
- ❏ antihistamines
- ❏ decongestants
- ❏ tweezers for disengaging ticks
- ❏ Sawyer Venom Extractor kit for stings and snake bites

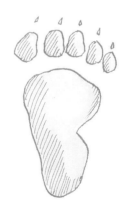

APPENDIX 4

CLEANING AND STORING GEAR

Because you have invested a lot of money and energy in your backpacking gear, you'll want to spend some time maintaining it. Cleaning your gear after backpacking trips and storing it properly will keep it performing well and will make it last longer. A little effort when you return from a trip will save you the agony of replacing gear or having an item break when you're in the backcountry. Follow these guidelines to keep your gear in good condition.

Backpacks

After each use, shake debris out of each compartment and clean the dirt off your pack with a soft brush and mild detergent. Clean the zippers and lubricate them with silicone spray. Inspect the seams, straps, and buckles for any signs of fraying or weakening. Fix them before they become a problem.

Make sure the pack is dry before you store it. Also, remove all food from the pack. Mice will chew through the nylon to get at anything that smells like food. Store the pack in a cool, dry, dark place because direct sunlight will eventually weaken nylon.

Boots

Clean your boots regularly. Dirt and grime will dry out leather and synthetic materials, causing them to crack and deteriorate. Use water and a good scrubber to clean your boots. After cleaning, remove the footbeds and let them air-dry. Treat leather boots with a silicone-based conditioner or waterproofing treatment to keep them functioning properly. Whatever you do, don't expose your boots to a heat source like a radiator or a campfire. Direct heat may melt or burn the materials that are holding the boot together. Store boots in a dry, cool place.

Tents

During a hike, pitch your tent in the shade if at all possible. Ultraviolet radiation will deteriorate the tent fabric. Before you pack up, shake any debris out of the tent. Before you store it, let it dry completely. Mildew can form within forty-eight hours, and once it's there, you can't get rid of it.

At home, clean the tent by wiping it down with a wet cloth and letting it air-dry. When you store the tent for a night or for the winter, stuff it into its stuff sack. Avoid folding the tent like a blanket; material that is repeatedly creased in the same place will weaken and the water-resistant coating may crack. I put the poles in first, then methodically stuff the tent, then the rainfly, into the stuff sack. A little disorder is good for the tent, and it's much easier to stuff it without folding it.

Sleeping Bags

Dirt and body oils will eventually work their way into the fill, so try to keep your bag as clean as possible. Change into clean clothes and give yourself a wipe-down (especially if you've applied bug repellent or sunscreen during the day) before you hit the sack.

You can wash a synthetic-filled sleeping bag in a front-loading washing machine and dry it in a dryer on low heat. Because down-filled bags may lose some of their insulating properties when they're washed, only wash a down bag when you absolutely have to. It's best to wash a down bag by hand in a bathtub and dry it in a dryer. Avoid dry-cleaning any sleeping bag; most cleaning solvents will strip down's natural oils and destroy synthetic fibers.

Make sure your bag is completely dry before stuffing it in its sack. On the trail, unzip the bag and let it dry while you eat breakfast. There is no need to roll the bag; stuff it in the stuff sack in clumps, as you do the tent.

Never store a sleeping bag in its stuff sack for long periods. Keep it in a large storage sack to avoid crushing the fill material. Do everything you can to maintain your bag's loft (or fluffiness), for it is the loft that will keep you warm. Many bags come with a large cotton storage sack. You can also store it on a closet shelf or on a hanger.

Sleeping Mattresses

Wash your inflatable mattress with a mild detergent and water to remove dirt, insect repellent, and sunscreen, all of which can damage the material. If your mattress gets wet on a trip, prevent mildew by unrolling it and letting it dry as soon as you get home. Don't leave your sleeping pad in direct sunlight for extended periods. Store an inflatable mattress unrolled with the valve open. Keep it in a dry, cool place, and don't pile anything on top of it that could puncture the pad.

Water Filters

Filters vary from model to model, so follow the cleaning instructions that come with your water filter. Some filters come with a small cleaning brush. Other filters require that the filter cartridge be replaced from time to time.

Before storing a filter for long periods, put a capful of bleach in a quart jug and filter the water. The bleach will prevent microorganisms from multiplying on the filter while it's being stored. Make sure all the water is out of the filter and the tubes before you pack it up.

Stove

Carefully read the instructions that came with your stove, and follow the cleaning and storing guidelines that the manufacturer suggests. Always wipe dirt or spilled food off the stove after each use. Most stoves require that you clean the fuel line and jet from time to time to keep it from clogging. Detach the pump assembly from the fuel bottle (on liquid fuel stoves) before storing it to prevent a buildup of lacquer in the fuel line. Store your stove and unused fuel in a cool, dry place.

APPENDIX 5

RESOURCES

Books

Backcountry Cooking

Barker, Harriett. *The One-Burner Gourmet.* Chicago: Contemporary, 1981.

Brunell, Valerie, and Ralph Swain. *Wilderness Ranger Cookbook: A Collection of Backcountry Recipes by U.S. Forest Service Wilderness Rangers.* Helena MT: Falcon, 1990.

Fleming, June. *The Well-Fed Backpacker.* New York: Vintage, 1986.

Kesselheim, Alan. *Trail Food: Drying and Cooking Food for Backpacking and Paddling.* Camden ME: Ragged Mountain Press, 1998.

Miller, Dorcas S. *Good Food for Camp and Trail: All-Natural Recipes for Delicious Meals Outdoors.* Boulder CO: Pruett, 1993.

Map and Compass

Fleming, June. *Staying Found: The Complete Map and Compass Handbook.* Seattle: Mountaineers, 1994.

Kjellstrom, Bjorn. *Be Expert with Map and Compass: The Complete Orienteering Handbook.* New York: Macmillan, 1994.

Seidman, David, and Paul Cleveland. *The Essential Wilderness Navigator.* 2nd ed. Camden ME: Ragged Mountain Press, 2001.

Minimum-Impact Techniques

Harmon, Will. *Leave No Trace: Minimum Impact Outdoor Recreation.* Helena MT: Falcon, 1997.

McGivney, Annette. *Leave No Trace: A Practical Guide to the New Wilderness Ethic.* Seattle: Mountaineers, 1998.

Meyer, Kathleen. *How to Shit in the Woods: An Environmentally Sound Approach to a Lost Art.* 2nd ed., rev. Berkeley: Ten Speed Press, 1994.

Expanding Your Horizons

Gabbard, Andrea. *Mountaineering: A Woman's Guide.* Camden ME: Ragged Mountain Press, 1999.

Ganci, Dave. *Desert Hiking.* Berkeley: Wilderness Press, 1993.

Gorman, Stephen. *AMC Guide to Winter Camping: Wilderness Travel and Adventure in the Cold-Weather Months.* Boston: Appalachian Mountain Club Books, 1991.

Graydon, Don, and Kurt Hanson, eds. *Mountaineering: The Freedom of the Hills.* Seattle: Mountaineers, 1997.

Hall, Adrienne. *A Journey North: One Woman's Story of Hiking the Appalachian Trail.* Boston: Appalachian Mountain Club Books, 2000.

Hall, Adrienne. *Backpacking: A Woman's Guide.* Camden ME: Ragged Mountain Press, 1998.

Houston, Charles S. *Going Higher: Oxygen, Man, and Mountains.* Seattle: Mountaineers, 1998.

Mueser, Roland. *Long-Distance Hiking: Lessons from the Appalachian Trail.* Camden ME: Ragged Mountain Press, 1998.

Townsend, Chris. *Wilderness Skiing and Winter Camping.* Camden ME: Ragged Mountain Press, 1994.

Safe Travels

Armstrong, Betsy R., and Knox Williams. *The Avalanche Book.* Rev. ed. Golden CO: Fulcrum, 1992.

Bezruchka, Stephen. *Altitude Illness: Prevention and Treatment: How to Stay Healthy at Altitude—From Resort Skiing to Himalayan Climbing.* Seattle: Mountaineers, 1994.

Breyfogle, Newell D. *Commonsense Outdoor Medicine and Emergency Companion.* 3rd ed. Camden ME: Ragged Mountain Press, 1993.

Brown, Gary. *Safe Travel in Bear Country.* New York: Lyons & Burford, 1996.

Wilkerson, James A. *Medicine for Mountaineering and Other Wilderness Activities.* 4th ed. Seattle: Mountaineers, 1992.

Take the Family

Doan, Marlyn. *The Sierra Club Family Outdoors Guide: Hiking, Backpacking, Camping, Bicycling, Water Sports, and Winter Activities with Children.* San Francisco: Sierra Club Books, 1994.

Euser, Barbara J. *Take 'Em Along: Sharing the Wilderness with Your Children.* Evergreen CO: Cordillera Press, 1987.

Gordon, Herb. *The Joy of Family Camping.* Short Hills NJ: Burford Books, 1998.

Ross, Cindy, and Todd Gladfelter. *Kids in the Wild.* Seattle: Mountaineers, 1995.

Silverman, Goldie. *Backpacking with Babies and Small Children: A Guide to Taking the Kids Along on Day Hikes, Overnighters, and Long Trail Trips.* Berkeley: Wilderness Press, 1998.

You and Your Pooch

Hoffman, Gary. *Happy Trails for You and Your Dog: What You Really Need to Know When Taking Your Dog Hiking or Backpacking.* Riverside CA: Insight Out, 1996.

Lerner, Richard. *Hiking with Your Dog.* Birmingham: Menasha Ridge Press, 1994.

Mullally, Linda B. *Hiking with Dogs: Becoming a Wilderness-Wise Dog Owner.* Helena MT: Falcon, 1999.

Smith, Cheryl S. *On the Trail with Your Canine Companion: Getting the Most Out of Hiking and Camping with Your Dog.* New York: Howell Book House, 1996.

Map Resources

ESIC Headquarters
U.S. Geological Survey
507 National Center
Reston VA 20192
888-ASK-USGS (888-275-8747)
http://ask.usgs.gov

Western Mapping Center, ESIC
U.S. Geological Survey
345 Middlefield Rd.
Menlo Park CA 94025
415-329-4309
www-wmc.wr.usgs.gov

Rocky Mountain Mapping Center, ESIC
U.S. Geological Survey
P.O. Box 25286
Denver CO 80225
800-435-7627
http://rockyweb.cr.usgs.gov

Mid-Continent Mapping Center, ESIC
U.S. Geological Survey
1400 Independence Rd.
Mailstop 231
Rolla MO 65401
573-308-3500
http://mcmcweb.er.usgs.gov/

DeLorme Mapping Co.
P.O. Box 298
Yarmouth ME 04096
207-846-7000
www.delorme.com

Earthwalk Press
5432 La Jolla Hermosa Ave.
La Jolla CA 92037
800-828-6277
www.globecorner.com/s/400.html
www.omnimap.com/catalog/cats/earthwal.htm

Trails Illustrated
P.O. Box 4357
Evergreen CO 80437-4357
800-962-1643, 303-670-3457
www.trailsillustrated.com

Wilderness Press
1200 5th St.
Berkeley CA 94710
800-443-7227, 510-558-1666
www.wildernesspress.com

Wilderness Medicine Courses

Stonehearth Open Learning Opportunities (SOLO)
P.O. Box 3150
Conway NH 03818
603-447-6711
www.stonehearth.com

Wilderness Medicine Institute
P.O. Box 9, 413 Main St.
Pitkin CO 81241
970-641-3572
www.wildernessmed.com

Wilderness Medical Associates
189 Dudley Rd.
Bryant Pond ME 04219
888-WILD MED (888-945-3633), 207-665-2707
www.wildmed.com

National Association for Search and Rescue
4500 Southgate Pl., Suite 100
Chantilly VA 20151-1714
703-222-6277
www.nasar.org

Long-Distance Trail Organizations

American Discovery Trail Society
P.O. Box 20155
Washington, DC 20041-2155
800-663-2387, 703-753-0149
E-mail: adtsociety@aol.com
www.discoverytrail.org/

Appalachian Trail Conference
P.O. Box 807
Harpers Ferry WV 25425
304-535-6331
E-mail: info@atconf.org
www.atconf.org
www.appalachiantrail.org

Colorado Trail Foundation
710 10th St., #310
Golden CO 80401-1022
303-384-3729
E-mail: ctf@coloradotrail.org
www.coloradotrail.org

Continental Divide Trail Alliance
P.O. Box 628
Pine CO 80470
888-909-CDTA (888-909-2382), 303-838-3760
E-mail: cdnst@aol.com
www.cdtrail.org

Continental Divide Trail Society
3704 N. Charles St., #601
Baltimore MD 21218-2300
410-235-9610
E-mail: cdtsociety@aol.com
www.gorp.com/cdts/

Florida Trail Association
5415 S.W. 13th St.
Gainesville FL 32608
800-343-1882
www.florida-trail.org/

Ice Age Park and Trail Foundation
207 E. Buffalo St., Suite 515
Milwaukee WI 53202-5712
800-227-0046, 414-278-8518
E-mail: iat@execpc.com
www.iceagetrail.org/

Natchez Trace Trail Conference
P.O. Box 1236
Jackson MS 39152
601-373-6244
E-mail: jhodonttc@aol.com

North Country Trail Association
49 Monroe Center, Suite 200B
Grand Rapids MI 49503
888-454-NCTA (888-454-6282), 616-454-5506
E-mail: NCTAssoc@aol.com
www.northcountrytrail.org

Pacific Crest Trail Association
5325 Elkhorn Blvd., PMB #256
Sacramento CA 95842-2526
916-349-2109
E-mail: info@pcta.org
www.pcta.org/

Potomac Heritage National Scenic Trail
National Park Service
P.O. Box B
Harpers Ferry WV 25425
304-535-4014
E-mail: phnst@nps.gov
www.nps.gov/pohe/

National Organizations

American Hiking Society
1422 Fenwick Ln.
Silver Spring MD 20910
301-565-6704
E-mail: info@americanhiking.org
www.americanhiking.org/

American Trails
P.O. Box 11046
Prescott AZ 86304
520-632-1140
E-mail: AmTrails@future1.com
www.outdoorlink.com/amtrails
www.americantrails.org

Appalachian Long-Distance Hikers Association
10 Benning St., PMB 224
West Lebanon NH 03784
E-mail: aldha@connix.com
www.aldha.org/

Appalachian Mountain Club
5 Joy St.
Boston MA 02108
617-523-0636
E-mail: information@amcinfo.org
www.outdoors.org

National Audubon Society
700 Broadway
New York NY 10003
212-979-3000
E-mail: chadd@audubon.org
www.audubon.org

The Nature Conservancy
4245 N. Fairfax Dr.
Arlington VA 22203
800-628-6860
www.tnc.org

The Sierra Club
85 2nd St., 2nd Floor
San Francisco CA 94105-3441
415-977-5500
E-mail: information@sierraclub.org
www.sierraclub.org/

Products

Counter Assault
120 Industry Ct.
Kalispell MT 59901
800-695-3394
www.counterassault.com
Pepper spray for wildlife attacks.

N/R Laboratories, Inc.
900 E. Franklin St.
Centerville OH 45459
800-223-9348, 937-433-9570
Fax 937-433-0779
www.norinse.com
No-rinse shampoo and other products.

Useful Web Sites

American Hiking Society,
www.americanhiking.org

American Park Network,
www.americanparknetwork.com

Appalachian Trail Conference Trail Resource Links,
www.atconf.org/hike/links.html

Appalachian Trail Homepage Trail Links,
www.fred.net/kathy/at/otherlinks.html

Backpacker Magazine, *www.bpbasecamp.com*

Backpacker Network, *www.thebackpacker.net*

Great Outdoors Recreation Pages, *www.gorp.com*

U.S.D.A. Forest Service, *www.fs.fed.us*

INDEX

Numbers in **bold** refer to pages with illustrations